Step Into Your Power

Step Into Your Power

STUDY JOURNEY

A 'JEREMIAH 9 WOMAN' SERIES

MICHELLE RHNEA YISRAEL

Registered in the United States Library of Congress

ISBN 978-1-951667-29-0

Dear Heavenly Father,

Bless the study journey of the readers who embark on this journey. Recharge their soul and renew their hope. Please go before them. Clear the way and protect them. Bring the right people into their lives and move the wrong people out of the way. Guide them with your love and give them your joy. Bring gratitude and joy the heart of the readers of this book.

In Christ name, Jesus the Christ's name, Yahushua ha Messiah,

Amen.

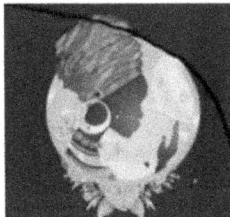

Table of Contents

1

My Personal Testimony

I would like to give honor to the Godhead, The True and Living God and His son Christ. Become a Praying Woman was the first in the Jeremiah 9 Woman series and was written to help women begin their prayer journey. Step Into Your Power is written to help you learn to grow in your gifts and skills; take a class, earn a certificate or degree, and grow your talents while you patiently wait.

"In the middle of difficulty lies opportunity"
-Albert Einstein

"When we long for life without difficulties, remind us that oaks grow strong in contrary winds and diamonds are made under pressure"
-Peter Marshall

Zechariah 13:9, "And I will bring the third part through the fire, and will refine them as silver is refined, and will try them as gold is tried: they shall call on my name, and I will hear them: I will say, It is my people: and they shall say, The LORD is my God."

Ephesians 5:19, "Speaking to yourselves in psalms and hymns and spiritual songs, singing and making melody in your heart to the Lord;"

As our five children grew and we survived their teen years, and they went off to college. I counted down. One down, four to go. Two down, three to go. Three down, two to go, I counted. Finally, they were all gone off to college, finished their degree or certificate program and graduated. They started their first career, experienced job struggles, and had challenging relationships. Every parent-adult child relationship experiences a profound change between college graduation and the "pay your own rent" season. This individual, who has progressed from an underfoot toddler to tumultuous teen, is abruptly out the door, certain that they have all they need to be a "grown-up." As you see them confidently march on, you realize they have no idea you are trying to figure out how to be a mother of adults.

It probably took me too long to figure out how to hold my peace and refrain from giving advice unless I am asked. Many times, I wanted to intervene because I thought I understood my children their personalities, and their character. I doubled my efforts to be kind, gentle, and patient toward them since my days of providing for them, educating them, disciplining them, reprimanding them, and directing them was long gone. It took too long for me to realize that the best thing I could do for my sons and daughters was to commit to prayer. I learned just as my parents had to step back and allow me to learn life lessons from my mistakes, I had to do the same thing with my adult children. Nevertheless, I've spent the previous 18+ years preparing them for this transition.

During a fall holy day season when I was home alone and each of the children were away either at school or working in other states, I felt compelled to increase the length and earnestness of my prayers for my children. One day that compulsion grew to such a degree that I was determined to pray for my son who had struggles I could do nothing about, until I came to a sense of assurance that God would provide the guidance and deliverance he needed in my stead. When I wasn't working, I locked myself in the house and for days pleaded with God that would extend mercy to my adults as they hallowed out a place for themselves in this world. I believed that God would answer their prayers, if only I was sure they were praying and following Him. My heart pleaded with Him to make them pray to Him. It was through prayer that I have less and less of physiological reaction the permeates throughout my body when I learn of a challenge my children go through. It was through the pleading of a mother for her children that God taught me through His word to use praise as a tool and weapon. I learned to worship God that season and my faith increased. I knew that He heard me and I knew just as He taught me to pray and praise Him, He had the power to do the same for my children. Prayer helped me to link my heart to God's purpose as a praying mother for my adult children. By praying over them, I put my worries in God's capable hands and build my faith that He would provide for them as He provided for me. Step Into Your Power is my reflections on what I learned as I embarked on my journey to become a praying mother.

I was reminded of the quote by Peter Marshall and looked at my children as strong oak trees and "oaks grow strong in contrary winds and diamonds are made under pressure." God can't strengthen my children's character without storms and sometimes fire brought about by those storms. In the middle of difficulties being a mother of adult children, I found the need to increase my faith and further develop my personal prayer life. Don't get me wrong, it was not easy as I grew in understanding prayer, and it is not easy now. I am still "becoming" more and more, better and better each day. My growth is continuous; I never know enough. Speaking to myself in psalms, hymns, and spiritual songs and melodies relieves me of the physiological irritation when I know my children are going through a storm. As we are all refined as silver like all God's servants, and when they hurt, I hurt. When I pray, meditate, and praise, I hurt less.

As we are in the process of raising our children, we think life will get easier when our children are grown. This is a chief contradiction for a praying mother. It is when our children are adults where our knees meet the floor the most. The stress of listening to the trials and tribulation of adult children and watching their struggles and chastisement can kill a mother as fast as a bullet. It truly defines the common phrase, "they are God's children, given to me on loan." Mothers must find our peace by trusting in God so we can enjoy the joy for living that only comes from God.

Zechariah 13:9, "And I will bring the third part through the fire, and will refine them as silver is refined, and will try them as gold is tried: they shall call on my name, and I will hear them: I will say, It *is* my people: and they shall say, The LORD *is* my God."

A mother's prayer is a powerful tool, as she communicates with God about her child's situation. It's a reassurance that God is already aware of the situation, and her prayer is a way of aligning her heart with His.

A praying mother understands her limitations. She will try her best to fix her child's situations that are under her control, but she also understands her limitations regarding those things in which she has no control. She knows that her only role is very often to pray and possibly encourage if the occasion occurs. This understanding brings her peace and reassurance, knowing that she can show your children how to touch and feel God and love and worship Him by her example. She can model the necessary behavior to her children.

A parent's heart is connected to God's purpose and design through prayer for our adult children. Praying over them increases our faith that God is our source and it releases our worries into His capable hands. Prayer, meditation, and praise connects our hearts for our adult children to the divine plan of God. Praying over them releases a parent's anxieties into His capable hands, and establishes our confidence that He will provide, direct, teach, and protect them.

A Reflective Study

Let's grow in God and grow in both womanhood and sisterhood with the Jeremiah 9 Woman series, a commitment to growing beyond the basics we get in class. These studies are self-directed and self-paced and will help us rise up to be the praying women we were meant to be. In this series, we will grow together and discover the traits of the growing Godly woman and how we can apply them to our lives. The Jeremiah 9 Woman series will help women see themselves in Bible literature. This book will help those in need of help in their unique and exquisite singleness and those sisters who need support in building a beautiful single woman and nurturing healthy marriages.

To be totally committed to God is the best definition of a woman of God, so she won't be overly concerned about how others see her actions when she is always focused on doing what He would want her to do. In this definition, she uses the gifts, skills, and talents with which HE has endowed her to benefit HIM. **1 Corinthians 12:7** says, "But the manifestation of the Spirit is given to every man to profit withal." In this manifestation, given to a woman of God, it is used for the common good of those around her. The prototypes of a woman of God within this simple definition are vast. One thing for certain is that each of the women in the three prototypes work to change, develop, and build her heart into a being whose heart, rather than outward appearance, is beautiful according to the standards dictated to her by God in his Word. **1 Samuel 16:7** says, "But the LORD said unto Samuel, Look not on his countenance, or on the height of his stature; because I have refused him: for the LORD seeth not as man seeth; for man looketh on the outward appearance, but the LORD looketh on the heart."

Although it is also good to take care of your temple by keeping it clean, groomed, and healthy, she will love Christ and obey His commandments **John 14:15**. As in **John 13:34**, the Woman of God will actively love other Israelite Christians and those of other persuasions. She learns from her mistakes and rarely repeats them intentionally; rather, she uses the Word as her reproof **2 Timothy 3:16**. She will exhibit the fruit of the Spirit, **Galatians 5:22–23**, in all her life. The most important character trait of a woman of God is the inward attitude that causes her to submit to God in all she does as a child of light, **Ephesians 5:8**.

We all have storms in our lives that often seem to be a personal attack. Never forget that God is bigger than the storm. Remember the story of the disciples being scared of a pretty bad storm and Jesus woke up to quiet it. They seemed offended that he was resting during the storm while they were full of fear. This story is a good example of the thin line between fear and faith. "And he arose, and rebuked the wind, and said unto the sea, Peace, be still. And the wind ceased, and there was a great calm. And he said unto them, why are ye so fearful? how is it that ye have no faith? And they feared exceedingly, and said one to another, What manner of man is this, that even the wind and the sea obey him?" **Mark 4: 39-41**. The storms we face seem to be a distraction to get us to faint so we don't get to reap the harvest. **Galatians 6:9**, And let us not be weary in well doing: for in due season we shall reap, if we faint not." Paul urged the Galatians to continue doing good during a time when Galatian Christians were not being so neighborly to one another. Doing good takes effort, especially during life's storms and when one questions whether it is worthwhile. Paul encourages the Galatians to continue living by their beliefs. They are free in Christ, and God's Spirit is among them. And remember, the promise of eternal life is not just a hope, but a certainty. Eventually, the harvest of perpetual life will appear, and people will witness for themselves. It is important for our salvation that women see themselves in the Bible so they can whether the storms, push past them to reap the benefits of salvation.

Biblical Prototypes for Women of God

It is important for everyone to see themselves in literature in order to fully relate to it on a deep level so that it permeates our being down to the cellular level in order for us to draw close to God in the way advised in **James 4:8**. Additionally, **Jeremiah 31:22** provides a hint of our role and responsibility. "How long wilt thou go about, O thou backsliding daughter? for the Lord hath created a new thing in the earth, A woman shall compass a man." In this passage, we are judged because giving the faults of the men to God is not what we do naturally. It also offers hope at the same time. The passage conveys a message of hope and restoration to the people of Israel while directing women and showing us part of the role of a woman of God. To compass a man means to press around her physical husband and her divine husband instead of shyly or angrily keeping a standoffish attitude or remaining indifferent, even when we feel like our emotional, physical, and spiritual needs are not met. It helps to pray about it, "Lord help me be the woman that you want me to be. Help me do what I need to do and change in the way I need to change in order to save myself from this untoward generation and make my calling and election sure."

There are few places in the Bible where we get a glimpse of things that describe a woman of Godly character. **Proverbs 31:10-31**, **Titus 2:3-5**, and **Jeremiah 9:17-20** are three that stand out as prototypes. These scriptural prototypes provide an far-reaching depiction that makes even the godliest of women feel either discouraged and overwhelmed or encouraged and empowered. I encourage all women to promote themselves by keeping their eye on the Word of God, looking at their lives, and analyzing how they live out the essence of their womanhood in the world, especially in their circle.

The *Proverbs 31 woman* is a married sister who focuses on ensuring her family has what they need. She is a good helper to her husband who trusts her to do business and make important decisions. She fulfilled needs of everyone in her family and community including her own. We have as our examples the Proverbs 31 woman, in our circles, who are busy taking care of the needs of her family from sun up to sun down. When I read about the Proverbs 31 woman, I think God wants His daughters to model serving Him with all their heart, soul, and mind. She is a model for helping a husband, nurturing children, serving others, and conducting business. She is strong, honorable, hard-working, hospitable, and full of good works. She is a stick of dynamite, the ambitious one, the nurturing, caring one, the extremely busy one with no time for idle distractions. She needs the *Jeremiah 9 Women* and the *Titus 2 Women* in her circle to keep her in their prayers as she does the work of The Lord and propels forward in her ministry. She has to be mindful that we are not performing the "work" for the sake of getting approval of people around us. She has to mindful to practice intentional self-care so she won't become an unhealthy workaholic.

The *Jeremiah 9 Woman* is the second prototype for women of God in the book. The bible describes her as a wise woman who is cunning or skillful in prayer. God refused to hear the unrepentant prayers of men of the time and suggested they call for women whom he knew prayed to him constantly, to pray for them. These were women who had experienced great loss and were conditioned to cry and pray to God. He told the men to have these praying women pray for the nation. These women cried for the desperation of Israel because of the torment they faced because of the nation's sin against God. The scripture makes no mention of the marital status, age, or occupations of these cunning praying women who were accustomed to crying out to God for the nation. In her thoughts of prayer, she adds power to her life. We have as our example the Jeremiah 9 Woman vs 17-20 who obviously on her knees praying constantly, otherwise how would God know them as cunning wailing women. Not only were they praying women but they were wailing women, crying to The Lord of Host for herself, her family and her nation. According to that passage she used her intense crying in a cunning way to get The Lord's attention. Wailing - A loud drawn out scream or howl. Cunning - skillful, artful, proficiency.

Note in **Jeremiah 9:17-20** there was not only one sister whom God called to pray there was a group of them. How big a group? The passage does not say, we know there were at least two or there could have been 10, 50, who knows? The number of women he called doesn't matter actually but what does matter is:

- How many women can he find now,
- Will you be part of the number?
- Will he look at you when he calls women to pray for our nation?
- What characters can you imagine he saw in those women?

I assume the women of God are called to pray often, how else would God see the women could get the job done. If you want to be a Jeremiah 9 Woman, today let him see you too can get the job done. Pick a time or two and pray for the people around you. Pray for the righteous to be surrounded....to be surrounded by God's hedges and pray for the unrighteous to hear and change, pray for the healing of the sick, and for God's will to be done so they can flee to the place of safety. Don't forget to add praise to your prayer. Praise God that He is the same yesterday and today and forever, **Hebrews 13:8**, and that He is your solid Rock, your Fortress, your Rescuer, your Shield, your salvation's strength, and your current place of safety, **Psalm 18:2**. Let Him see you praying every day so that when He calls for the cunning wailing women to pray. He calls you.

The *Titus 2 Woman* is an elder sister, the last prototype of women of God, who is an excellent example and teacher to young women. A Titus 2 woman is an "oldish" women, the elderly women who were probably at some time in their lives a proverbs 31 woman, applying the Word in every aspect of their lives, taking care of her family's needs, teaching her children to serve the True and Living God, submitting to a husband who was, I hope, a man of God, submitting to God's son and striving to be like Christ. But if you have a husband who is not striving to be like Christ, my sister, start today and stay on your knees building your craft, become a praying woman, increase your ability to pray cunningly to your God to fix things, because He can. There is no situation that is impossible for God. A Titus 2 woman has to be spirit-empowered, faith-cultivated, and delight in love-based sister in order to be effective in her role as a mentor.

As a young woman, she had to be one who has learned to be a Proverbs 31 Woman to her husband, her family, and her community, or have survived a difficult marriage without becoming mean and bitter about life. She had to have learned to love her children, and have learned to be reverent, godly, modest and wise. The Titus 2 Woman may have been a Jeremiah 9 Woman because to be a good mentor of young women, she has to be a praying woman. Titus 2 Women are charged with seeking out and mentoring a younger woman who crosses her path. She is a mentor and shares her experiences and understanding with them.

Reflection: Reflecting on Three Prototypes for Women

Proverbs 31:10-31; Jeremiah 9:17-20; Titus 2:3-5.
(*Worksheets are in Chapter 8 Useful Tools*)

Remembering, Comprehending & Applying

1. What are the virtues of a Proverbs 31 woman as described in the passage?
2. Write a description of what a Proverbs 31 woman might look like in today's world.
3. What are the attributes of a Titus 2 woman as described in the passage?
4. Write a description of what a Titus 2 woman might look like in today's world.
5. What are the characteristics of a Jeremiah 9 woman as described in the passage?
6. Write a detailed description of what a Jeremiah woman might look like in today's world.
7. How can the characteristics of each woman of God be summed up in a few sentences?
8. As you begin a personal purge, what do you want to learn from each of these prototypes?
9. How did these women grow in the fruits of the spirit?
10. How do we assume each prototype wears the garment of salvation,

the robe of righteousness, and other parts of the armor willingly and even joyfully?

ANALYZING, EVALUATING & SYNTHESIZING

11. What can you infer from the directive that God gave the Jeremiah 9 woman to teach her daughters?
12. What kind of love does each prototype demonstrate?
13. We can also do a deeper dive into certain specific words like the meaning of "submit" or "love".
14. Compare and contrast the 3 prototypes.
15. What consistent pattern of behavior does God see in your daily walk that could cause God to call you when he calls for women to pray?
16. How does each prototype present us with a list that challenges our actions, our integrity, and our daily walk?
17. Which prototype do you identify with or aspire to be? Why?
18. What purging have you done so far?
19. What further purging do you need to do?
20. What will be your process for growth to reach the depths of the prototype you selected?

REFLECTION: CONTINUOUS PERSONAL GROWTH

1. Write these prototypes for women at the top of a page in your notebook.
   a. Proverbs 31:10-31
   b. Jeremiah 9:17-20
   c. Titus 2:3-5
2. Now create a list of 5 or more characteristics for each prototype on the 3 pages. You want to see each clearly.
3. Next, which study the list of characteristics to determine which ones overlap. You can use a graphic organizer with 3 circles if you want.
4. Then write the characteristics which overlap on a separate page or a separate section of your notebook.
5. Self-Reflection: Analyze both lists as they pertain to you. Which characteristics from your lists have you already developed?
6. Which characteristics do you need to work on?
7. Then prioritize that list on which you need to work. Group them according to similarities and differences.

     a.   Can you work on any two or three one at a time?

     b.   Which do you need to work on alone?

     c.   Which will you start first?

8. Do you have forgiveness to do? What steps can we take to forgive whomever and let go? Which characteristics did you identify in the 3 prototypes will you develop automatically when you forgive?

9. Your final list should focus on things you can do to build your character as a woman of God and a value to your sisterhood.

Biblical Prototypes

Proverbs 31 Woman	Titus 2 Woman	Jeremiah 9 Woman
Household	Next Generation	Nation

2

Write the Vision, Make it Plain

Vision Board (Book) Activity

Build your foundations on prayer and the truths in God's Word. Use this vision board activity to increase the quality of your life and to build strong foundations for life today and in life to come. Let your goals to be the basis for developing your prayer life. Setting goals promotes self-reflection while promoting accountability and discipline. When you commit your goals to paper, you're making a promise to yourself. This commitment is a powerful motivator, pushing you to take consistent actions toward your goals. It's about being responsible for your basic human needs and recognizing that you can make significant changes in your life, leading to personal growth. Ultimately, these goals can be a source of immense empowerment, fueling your journey towards personal growth and success. Besides food, shelter, and clothing, humans have five basic needs: physical health, mental wellness, academic or career needs, social connections, and spiritual focus.

Physical Health Needs

We know physical health and wellness is important. Being physically healthy is crucial because it allows you to function at your peak in all aspects of your life. Physical wellness means eating a healthy and balanced diet, being physically active every day, getting adequate sleep, and having annual checkups with your doctor or natural health care practitioner.

Mental Wellness Goal

Gain clarity and confidence by setting mental health goals. This simple and effective step is your first move towards improved mental and emotional well-being. Mental health goals provide a focus, whether managing anxiety, boosting your mood, or building stronger relationships. A clear focus is essential for turning ambiguous goals into concrete results and providing a strong sense of direction, ensuring that you're headed in the right way regarding your mental health. Setting mental health goals is a journey of self-reflection. It's an opportunity to explore your innermost needs and desires, gaining a profound understanding of yourself and helping to rid yourself of depression and anxiety. Reading for relaxation, creating and crafting, and learning new things enhance mental wellness.

Academic or Career Goals

When you are productive, your general mental health and well-being may improve. Having a purpose behind work you are passionate about and being productive in it helps motivate you and keeps your mental health balanced.

Social Connections

Genuine face-to-face interactions nourishes the soul and fosters a sense of belonging. Family therapist Virginia Satir suggests, "We need 4 hugs a day for survival. We need 8 hugs a day for maintenance. We need 12 hugs a day for growth." Frequent hugs can boost physical health, lower blood pressure, release a feel-good hormone called serotonin, and lessen feelings of loneliness. Additionally, it raises our serotonin levels and causes oxytocin to be released over time, which affects us cellularly, elevating good feelings, bringing us into tune with life's energy, and reducing heart rate.

Spiritual Focus

The scriptures do not discourage preparation, but the most important thing we can prepare for the next life, eternity. Do not try to wait until you are near death because no one knows what a day may bring. Today is the time to prepare for your future on earth and the future life in New Jerusalem. What a magnificent thought! We can live well now and later. This is done by studying the word of God, understanding it, and applying it to your daily walk while serving others when and how you are able.

Vision Board Exercise, (also called Vision Book)

Before I explain what a spiritual vision board activity I should start by defining the definition I use for the word spiritual. Spirituality is the process of developing one's mindset and approaches, familial beliefs, worldviews, as well as morals and values from a biblical perspective. The foundation for this biblical perspective should not come from institutionalized religion, cultural, or tradition.

Have you ever created a vision board before? If you have, then you may understand how they help solidify your goals through visual representation. Vision boards speak to the subconscious mind, always reminding you of the path you want to manifest. As busy women, it's essential to be goal-oriented and focused. Without direction, many of our dreams and aspirations will fizzle and come to naught. But today you're going to put a stop to dead-end aspirations. Today, you will be empowered! Today, you will be successful. As a matter of fact, those are your first two affirmations for your vision board. It is suggested you add to or change appropriate portions of your vision board each time you begin one of the Jeremiah 9 Woman books in the series. You will be surprised at how you have changed, and your growth will be motivating. The vision boards become a window into your own soul.

What you will need: poster board or cork board, scissors, magazines, adhesive, photos, printed quotes, or affirmations. You can also create your vision board online using various tools, such as canva.com or fotor. com. The third option for your spiritual vision board is to create human needs on five 8 ½ x 11 card stock and organize the sheets in a 3-ring binder, there are many. Do a search for free vision board makers. Before you start your board or book, sit down, and write a list of all of your spiritual prayer goals. After you've compiled your list, then decipher which five goals require your immediate focus. Although this journey is a spiritual one, don't throw away your goals for education, business, travel. This vision board exercise is for you, so feel free to alter those established in this section of the book or other goals appropriate to your needs and desires. You decide which goals are important for you. When setting goals, it's imperative to make them attainable. Too many goals at once can be overwhelming, which is counterproductive to the whole process. Take it slow, so the process is sustainable. After you've picked out your immediate goals, find images, words, or quotes that represent them. These are the things that you will glue to your board. You can fill in the empty spaces with words of affirmation. Remember not to clutter your board or book. You want your board to be appealing and easy to read.

Once finished, stand your board up somewhere where it will get a lot of your attention. Places like in the bathroom next to where you brush your teeth or hang it where you can clearly see it as you take a long, hot bath. On a nightstand, or perhaps your desk. Wherever you decide to place it, select a place where you will want to look at it often and regularly. Add the things from your vision board into your prayer and meditation as you go through this study journey.

Monitoring Your Progress

Women of God need to be about continuous spiritual and emotional growth and in order to ensure that growth we need to monitor our progress. Monitoring your progress will help you understand how much you have grown in the process of becoming a Jeremiah 9 woman. Spend a designated number of minutes in the morning, the afternoon, and in the evening with Scripture — perhaps 15 - 20 minutes each studying the Word for the purpose of continuous growth and development. If you prefer, you can begin with your favorite books of the Bible.

You may want to consider reading the Old Testament in the morning, and the New Testament in the evening. The important thing is to set aside specific uninterrupted time and craft it into your schedule. When you study Tamar, Rahab, Ruth, and Bathsheba note these are imperfect women listed by name in the first chapter of Matthew in the genealogy of our Messiah. Why do you think it was important to mention these four imperfect women in the genealogy? It is interesting that Sarah, Rebekah, and Leah are not mentioned by name in his genealogy, their husbands are, so we know they are present.

JOURNAL ACTIVITY:

- Check in regularly. Create a timeline for yourself.
- Check it after every three months to chart your progress.
- Set your goals today for 1 week, one month, 6 months, and 1 year.
- Check your progress regularly and adjust where needed and appropriate.

As you participate in this self-reflective journey it may be beneficial to set aside some time to reconsider your actions and behaviors in your growth. This could include reflecting on past irregular spiritual and emotional patterns and identifying some of the things that have been challenging for you in the past as well as the things you need focus on in the present to ensure your future is spiritually and emotionally healthier. For example, you may understand that when your feelings are hurt, you prefer to withdraw from friends or family rather than seeking to speak and work through it. It may be beneficial to spend this time to reflect on whether your feelings have been wounded and how you handled that conflict.

Every relationship relies heavily on effective communication. It is critical to develop the ability to actively listen and communicate effectively. This could include creating clear boundaries with people, modulating your tone when someone offends you, and retaining information offered while showing you heard them with your actions. Each of these skills makes your loved ones feel cherished.

Feedback from family and friends is helpful in our spiritual and emotional growth. The most valuable insights about your relationships come from those you already know. Their perspective is crucial. It can be beneficial to initiate a talk about how your relationship has been affecting everyone involved. Consider asking questions like, "How has our relationship been feeling for you lately?" and "Is there anything I could be doing to show up for you more effectively?" These questions demonstrate your dedication to being a good friend for loving family member, which is an excellent place to begin. Feedback from friends is important because it holds us accountable and helps us grow in the weightier matters of the law, the fruits of the spirit.

3

The Jeremiah 9 Experience

Vision Board (Book) Activity

How do you join the Jeremiah 9 Movement? You join the movement by praying, meditating, studying, and placing yourself in environments where other praying women live, function, work, study, and grow.

To single sisters, don't move too fast. Pray to The Lord of Hosts for your Boaz to find you; it is his good thing. Be patient because before the Lord lets him see you, he's got to get his career together so the two of you build won't struggle. Pray he learns to lead, protect, and provide for you and your future children. If you have children coming into the relationship, pray that your husband loves your children as his own, and they will feel it. Pray he grows in love, patience, long-suffering, and kindness so he can be what you need to be a supportive, joyous, and submissive wife. Pray that the Lord rids his mind of anything that will cause you emotional distress. God knows you, and he knows your triggers and that he works through his trauma. When God is finished purifying him, he's going to be a good husband to you and an excellent father to his children. Pray now, before your husband finds you, and tell The Most High what you want in a husband so God can work on your Boaz so that when you come together, you can abide by the advice in Ephesians 5:21 and submit to one another. Enjoy your singleness while you pray and wait. Take a class, earn a degree or certificate, or learn a craft or trade. Use this time to build yourself and grow. Never stop praying and studying to show thyself approved of God.

To sisters experiencing a healthy marriage, praise God. You are among those sisters who have kind husbands growing in gentleness; it's beautiful. Remember to show gratitude for the blessing and pray for your husband. When you pray, God will enhance your marriage and deepen your love for one another as you seek his wisdom, favor, and protection. Prayer is an effective tool for gratitude and growth, and you may support your husband's spiritual development and the health of your marriage by continually bringing him up before the Lord. Incorporating prayers into daily routines can be a powerful tool for wives seeking to uplift their husbands and strengthen their marital bond. Prayer will help your husband grow in ways he needs to grow and be a better man of God than you could ever imagine. Prayer will change you so that you can better respect, support, encourage, and cherish your husband. Enjoy your marriage, be grateful, and continue to pray. God can make even a good thing better beyond your understanding.

To sisters who are not experiencing the joys of a healthy marriage, remember, God hates divorce, and it was not supposed to be, even from the beginning. Deuteronomy 24:1 and Mark 10:4 state God tolerates divorce because of hard hearts. As we know, we cannot leave our husbands for any reason. However, if you and or your children are in physical danger, you may have to come outside of the church for the help you need. However, while making necessary moves to escape for safety's sake, when needed, continue to pray, study, and keep your behavior aligned with The Most High. Understand fully, that being a single mother is very difficult. There are risks and there are difficulties. Whatever your decision, though, keep your garments clean. This is your saving grace.

- Text HOME to 741741 to reach a trained Crisis Counselor through Crisis Text Line, a global not-for-profit organization. Free, 24/7, confidential.
- Domestic Violence Helpline: The helpline is toll free, multilingual, and confidential. It is available 24-hours a day, 7 days a week.

1-877-TO END DV or 1-877-863-6338 (Voice), 1-877-863-6339 (TTY)
The helpline is toll free, multilingual, and confidential. It is available 24-hours a day, 7 days a week.

It is easier for sisters who have kind husbands with reasonable mindsets and are consciously growing in practicing the Word of God. We can easily be told to submit, which will resolve our issues. In solidarity, vulnerability, and accountability for your pain, "we" are obligated to ensure "us" and "our" children are physically safe. What about the children? I can attest that our children are forever scarred by what they see and hear in an abusive home. These scars are carried into their adulthood and into the relationships they have. You will see their pain in various ways based on their personalities and who they are. Considering what they are learning and experiencing is also up to you and your spouse.

In cases where you must make particular safety decisions, stay quiet, strategic, purposeful, and, above all, prayerful. HE provided a place for my children and me, and we lived there rent-free for 16 years afterward. Prayer is powerful and HE is a trustworthy provider. If you are physically safe, you can decide what you will submit to and what you will tolerate. Prayerfully, always pray, and never stop telling your Father in Jesus' name how you feel and why. HE cares and has the power to fix your situation and repair the breach and strengthen that three-fold cord of husband and wife. Just like HE stopped Paul in his tracks on the road to Damascus and asked him why he persecuted HIM, The Most High can do the same for any husband who is emotionally, verbally, financially, and even physically abusive.

God loves women, unlike popular belief. He did not cause us to be abused in any way. That was not HIS intention for us when HE created us. Even after Eve sinned and got Adam to partake, our part of our punishment was to be ruled over. Does rulership have to be complicated, brutal, and dictatorial? No. It does not. When husbands intentionally grow in the fruit of the spirit, they learn to rule in kindness and love. This way, submission is easy, the burden is light, and we submit naturally and willingly. I raise the question, does a husband who causes his wife pain and agony believe the word of God? Is he the unbelieving husband in 1 Corinthians 7:11-40? Can his believing wife sanctify him? That, my dear sister, is on a case-by-case basis. But don't be afraid to consult HIM and decide for yourself.

Talk to God and lean on HIM. Don't be scared to decide about your and your children's lives. When you focus on God and the things of Him, you will be made whole by His word. HE will uphold you, provide for you, heal you, and comfort you. HE will fix him or remove him. He has the power to do either, and HE will have mercy on you based on you and your integrity and submission to HIM. I know for a surety that a wife submitting to her husband is not always the answer in unhealthy homes. Be sure of your choice and pray about it again. Make sure you the green light from Go. We need another answer and a better solution. I read a post on Facebook saying, that if men would criticize and correct other men like they attempt to criticize and correct women, then the world would be better. When I read it, my heart leapt and I had the thought, "if they would encourage each other to get therapy and pray it would transform families." Instead generational trauma, hurt, and pain is passed from one generation to another, from one man to another from one woman to another and to our children, that our community does not stoop low enough to get therapy. We won't humble ourselves and talk to God, we are too busy to pray, or we are impatient for his answer. Well, how low do we need to go? Because of trauma forced on our ancestors, our grandfathers, our grandmothers and our parents, we need therapy more than any other community.

Again, don't listen to anyone's opinion—mine or others telling you to go or stay. How long should you pray and wait and live in pain? Five years, ten years, twenty years, or thirty? It is solely between you and your Father. I've known The Most High to change a brother or two, and they learned to love their wives because they learned to love and appreciate themselves. It could happen. There is always hope for change.

You have the power to decide whether you stay or go or how much you will tolerate. Cry your painful tears to The Most High, cry loud and cry often, but keep your decision between you and Him and walk in it. HE will carry you because you leaned on HIM, your first husband. He's kind, loving, and protective. Talk to HIM and trust your decision because you consulted HIM. However, based on your choice, understand you will lose friends you thought were dear. But remember, it's your life and your decision. And NO, you have no obligation to submit to abuse, whether physical, emotional, spiritual, or financial. You have the right to live in safety and respect, always. You have options because of your integrity with God and either way, the choice is yours. Choose prayerfully my dear sister.

There are sisters who have no desire to marry and that is okay too. There is no shame in that. Still, The True and Living God is your strength. Increase your prayer life so that your single-hood is healthy and you are wise in living it. Build your relationship with God. first and foremost. Make him the reason for your living. Grow in your gifts, skills and talents. Be mindful your peer group so that you don't "accidentally" get sucked into ways, events, and activities that are not of God. Pray for healthy friendships and familial relationships.

No matter your relationship status we should all be about self-reflection, healing, and restoration with God. Be confident, and study to show yourself approved of God. Learn to use your time off that God gave you, in **Leviticus 15:19**, "And if a woman have an issue, and her issue in her flesh be blood, she shall be put apart seven days: and whosoever toucheth her shall be unclean until the even," for physical and emotional self-care so you carry it into your marriage and are not overcome with the responsibilities of a Proverbs 31 woman. I talked more about this in Becoming a Praying Woman.

The Jeremiah 9 Woman movement is not revolutionary. Women have been putting on The Armour of God, growing in the Fruits of the Spirit, and being better at keeping the law for generations, loving God with all our hearts, souls, and might while loving others as we love ourselves. This is the formula for all servants of God and this is the what the Jeremiah 9 Woman Experience is about, this is how you draw close to God, step into your power to make your calling and election sure.

The Jeremiah 9 Movement is a revolution of praying women. Join the movement by praying continuously with a group of other praying sisters or alone. Give your anxiety over to God. Pray about your school life, career, and your relationships in your family, in your neighborhood and in your church community. Vet that man you are dating with prayer, BEFORE, you marry him so you will be a praying wife of a kind and gentle head who rules you under the gentle rulership of The Most High God. Be mindful and wait on the Lord. Being thirsty and inpatient will more than likely get you into an unstable and inappropriate situation. Once you move too quickly and the damage is done, you could be stuck with a brother who wreaks havoc on your life in ways you could never imagine right now. Jumping into relationships too quickly appears to be an epidemic in Israel. So, have patience and know your potential husband is from The Most High before you open yourself up to him.

A wise woman positions herself to ensure that those around her treat her with love and other fruits of the spirit. In the act of submission, a woman submits more effectively for the benefit of the partnership when her mate submits to Elohim. The spirit of God in your partner will draw you and allow submission to be natural and pleasurable. You should see the God in him, and submit to the God in him. You can easily follow when your husband leader gives you something fruitful to pursue. Women are natural responders; when we are loved, we respond with love, and we are not ashamed to love. The fruit of the Spirit is love, joy, peace, long-suffering, gentleness, goodness, faith, meekness, and temperance, according to **Galatians 5:22-23**. When you experience these fruits of Yah, then you can submit to leadership. Otherwise, your submission will feel uncomfortable and even painful. Prayer will help ensure your submission is fruitful, and you are not just giving yourself away for naught.

Some people say we should only pray in our closets, as the Messiah said in **Matthew 6:6**. If you choose to pray alone, there is nothing wrong with that. Find a quiet space where you can pray undisturbed. You can also pray in a group, as the apostles did in **Acts 4**. And whether we pray with a group of women or alone, there is a time where we are compelled by our feelings, experiences, and what goes on around us to pray either way, or both.

The Jeremiah 9 Woman Experience isn't revolutionary at all. For decades, women have put on God's armor, grown in the Fruits of the Spirit, and improved their ability to keep the law, loved God with all their hearts, souls, and might while loving others as they love themselves. This is the recipe for all those laboring for salvation. That is what the Jeremiah 9 Woman Experience is all about: stepping into your power to ensure your seat in the Kingdom of God. The fact that in **Jeremiah 9:17-20**, The

Most High suggested Jeremiah call for the cunning wailing women more than once in Jeremiah says praying in a group is also appropriate. According to **Matthew 18:20**, Jesus said, "For where two or three are gathered together in my name, there am I in the midst of them." We need community. "Community" is a concept for anyone interested in social change. There's something fascinating about the word "community." It exudes positivity and a sense of unity. It conveys a sense of both solidarity and familiarity. It is a useful tool to help shape our sense of what 'good' and 'bad' means and for socialization sake. We all need community, and a community of sisters can be very therapeutic.

Search your circle for a group of 3 -12 sisters with whom you can become a community of prayer partners and grow together. Join a sister's prayer circle that already exists or start one. Be open and creative. Before approaching your selections, pray about it so you can select sisters who are mature enough to learn how to become prayer intercessory women. Practice feeling or showing no judgment toward your prayer partner's confession. Being an intercessor is a serious responsibility. The women about whom we read in Jeremiah 9:17-20 are a community of prayer intercessors. Build your relationship with your sisters slowly, and let your community be based on The Word. your study, listening to one another, confessing sins and faults, praying, and praising The Father and His Son. Pray for the prayer community of your prayer partners and for the understanding of new information you have encountered in your studies. Meet in person or meet using an online tool. You and your prayer partners can decide when, where, and how regularly to meet.

Ensure your community of sisters is about love, prayer, praise, support, empathy, compassion, and all the fruit of the Spirit. Ward off gossip, judgment, jealousy, bullying, fear, anger, and all other emotions or actions that enter women's groups and are contrary to the Fruit of the Spirit and The Word of God. A Jeremiah 9 woman's group is not about reproving and rebuking one another. It is about using prayer to build oneself and one another. When reproof and rebuke are necessary, look in the mirror, then reprove and rebuke yourself. Your job is always to build, not tear down or rebuild one whom you have torn down. The tearing down and rebuilding is up to each individual. Jeremiah 9 also requires us to teach our daughters to pray. Think about how you will do that. If there are other daughters in your circle, think about how to organize them to teach them to pray. Being a Jeremiah 9 woman is a responsibility, more often than not, it requires you to think of others more than yourself.

Do not fret if there are no sisters around you. There are many women in The Word on most social networks who are also alone and would be willing to build a virtual prayer community with like minds, using phone conferencing. Be open, but be careful, and be willing to love from afar. Practice careful and selective efficacy. Sisters can form valuable connections with other sisters; it is necessary for this last part of the last days. Pray that you are influenced by righteous women and that you are able to influence them as well. We all have strengths; share them. We have areas of growth, share those too. Ask The Most High to help you select your circle. You can ask God anything. Remember, with God, all things are possible. **Matthew 19:23-30**.

When you identify your prayer circle, start your community by getting to know and understand what prayers each sister needs from you, and don't be ashamed to share your prayer request with them. Your sister's prayer circle is best for face to face prayer, at sessions set aside weekly or monthly. However, a distance prayer circle of sisters could also be effective if the sisters are honest, consistent, and value one another. Your community can be uplifting and motivating. Enjoy.

You will find a more detailed explanation of times to pray in the book in the Jeremiah 9 Series, Becoming a Praying Woman. To summarize it, women in your prayer group can divide the time among you and pray for the people in your circle at 6 p.m., 12 p.m., and 3 p.m. The first prayer of the day coincides with the morning sacrifice, at the 3rd hour of the morning, at 9 a.m. The second will be at the 6th hour, or at noon, and the time in this scripture may have coincided with the thanksgiving for the chief meal of the day, a custom apparently universally observed. The 3rd hour of prayer will coincide with the evening sacrifice, at the ninth hour, 3:00 P.M. **Matthew 15:36; Acts 27:35; Psalm 55:17; Acts 2:15. Acts 3:1** report that Peter and John went up together into the temple at the hour of prayer; which was the ninth hour, or three o'clock in the afternoon.

Remember, too, that Daniel prayed three times a day. I don't doubt there were women in the Bible who prayed as often or more. As a matter of fact, remember this conversation when you get to the study of the widow

Anna, who was in the temple praying all the time. The background story is that she married at fourteen years old, and seven years into her marriage, her husband died. **Luke 2:37**, "And she was a widow of about four hundred and four years, who departed not from the temple, but served God with fasting and prayers night and day." We don't know if she left her home and went into the temple daily or if she was given a room in the temple where she prayed day and night. What we do know is that she prayed night and day, to me, that means around the clock.

Your sister's prayer circle is a challenge for the women of God to pray round the clock for Israel, family, and friends worldwide while we are in this phase of pestilence. First payer responders are unsung heroes of our communities. They are always there when others need them, providing critical aid and comfort at all hours. Their confidence, consistency, and dedication deserve our deepest gratitude. They pray for wellness, healing, strength, protection, and peace in the lives of the people for all believers. Sometimes adding fasting, they tap into the power of God seeking supernatural power for others. We all need more prayer for protection as we approach the new year as The Most High sets the stage for the Abomination of Desolation and the new WORLD order as economics shift and heads of nations are brought to their knees. We see prophecy unfolding right before our eyes, we are living much of it. We know it is not the end yet, but with new pestilences, earthquakes in diverse places, and wars and rumors of wars, we can see the time of the end getting closer and closer. Pray that you and the sisters in your circle are able to put on the whole armor of God so we have His hedges of protection around us and can hear His message when it's time to flee to the place of safety He set up for His people in the day of destruction.

We know the plagues we encounter are just the beginning of sorrow. Pray, watch, and draw close to The Father and His son. Pray that we remain calm and true to His Word as world events begin to unfold. It's time to get right church, and let's go home. Faithful prayer with help us get there. What kept our ancestors safe as they prepared to flee Egypt will keep us safe as well. Faith and obedience to God's law while regularly keeping your heads in the scriptures is our map. Matthew 24 is a good start.

The Armour of God

The armor of God is a crucial concept to grasp and implement. It's not only for kids' coloring sheets, featuring an adorable soldier in full armor. After all, the Bible commands us to put on all of God's armor. The book of Ephesians is one of the most influential in the New Testament. You put on the whole armor of God by believing what God has done for you through Christ, the Messiah, and carrying out the elements of the armor in all aspects of your life. The complete armor of God is necessary to endure the spiritual pressures that you will be confronted with, sometimes daily.

Ephesians 6:14-17 explains the six components of God's armor. To put on the entire armor entails believing all Jesus has done as we read in Ephesians 6:1-3, In verses 1-5, obeying the Lord is following the commandments under the light of unity with The Most High. This unity extends from parents and children, to husband and wife, all in Christ. "This is right." refers to the order established by God, given to the children of Israel, and adopted by other nations, are divine and sanctioned in God's commandments. Wearing the armour is living in the power of God's actions in every aspect of life, beginning with the basic family structure, even when things are difficult and even when people in the world, like now, when people's behavior is reckless, impulsive, rash, and out of alignment with God's commandments.

In other words, to properly grasp the armor of God in Ephesians 6, you must first read Ephesians 1-5. It must be comprehended in its proper perspective. Putting on all of God's armor is more than just a method of focusing on darkness, evil, and spiritual warfare. It does not include a secret prayer, a profound spiritual experience, or visualization methods. Its connotation could be perceived as ambiguous; thus, many are unsure how to wear it. The Armor of God entails absorbing and utilizing everything God has done for you. The entire armor of God symbolizes your complete faith in God and all He has done for you via Jesus Christ, his life, his death, his resurrection, and the future job the Father has in store for him and those who trust him until the end. Your triumph in spiritual battle was achieved at Christ's crucifixion, and the bloodshed there, Revelation 12:11. The baptism disconnects you from your past battles and your daily walk after the baptism keeps you connected to salvation. The whole armor is designed to provide strength, stability, and encouragement, allowing you to receive whatever God has for you.

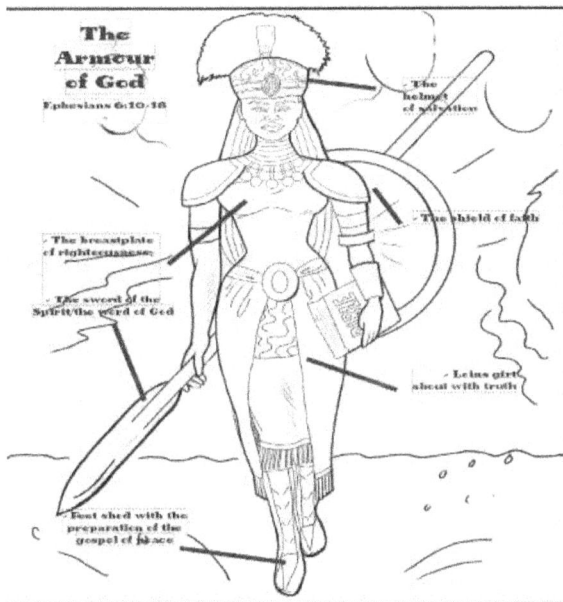

Illustration by Marguerite Wright

The Armour of God

From August 18-20, 2024, I conducted an informal survey of 100 sisters from different walks of Hebrew Israelite, Bible Christian, Messianic Israelite, Israelite Christian, and Traditional Christian life.

I asked, "How do you put on the armour of God? Basically, most sisters paraphrased the same strategies. It is great that despite our differences and the churches we attend, most women I surveyed agree about how to put on the armour of God. I did not get one response that was indecisive nor discordant or conflict-ridden. I was encouraged by the women's focus and these are a few responses I received.

"I put on the armour by reading the Word, discussing it, sometimes fasting and praying, collaborating or all three."

"I have had to establish a routine of daily prayer and study. I believe the gifts the Lord has blessed me with allow me to stay in the walk of faith. Giving back has always been in my heart, and the Lord has seen to it that

I am able to satisfy my desires which seem to align with His will. These daily routines help to me focused."

"I put on the armor of God by praying and fasting. Calling things out by name and girding my mind. I prepare my heart and mind through reading of his word and being vigilant for the times to come."

"I pray first and if that doesn't seem to help immediately, I study to ask for prayer and fasting. Fasting always helps with I am at my lowest. If prayer doesn't work immediately, it is because of my negative mindset at the time."

"I recommit to aligning my life with His Word daily. I ground myself in God's truth through prayer, mindfulness, and staying centered in His teachings. I strive to live righteously by judging my deeds according to His Word and self-correcting when I fall short. I understand that perfection is a goal to aspire to, not something we can achieved on our own. So I aim to make decisions that reflect His Word, continually striving toward it."

"By studying his word and keeping my mind on him, by allowing myself to stay around those things and people that are positive and following YAH, praying. (Need to do more fasting) Making sure that no matter what comes my way, I allow the Father to handle it. Understanding that no matter what the enemy hates me and if I'm not armored up, he'll annihilate me."

It's actually not as complicated as we sometimes make it out to be. It was exciting to get the sisters' texts, DM messages, emails, and comments in social media groups. I'll be excited to hug all these sisters in the wilderness. If we stay on the path, we are going to make it!

Ephesians 6:11-13, *"Put on the whole armour of God, that ye may be able to stand against the wiles of the devil. For we wrestle not against flesh and blood, but against principalities, against powers, against the rulers of the darkness of this world, against spiritual wickedness in high places. Wherefore take unto you the whole armour of God, that ye may be able to withstand in the evil day, and having done all, to stand."*

We begin each morning with God's weapons to combat the devil's wiles. We recognize that we are not fighting against individuals, even if they are present.

The struggle is with the principalities, powers, and rulers of the darkness of this world. We know precisely who the opponent is. We are aware of spiritual wickedness in high places, and the only way to compete is to put on God's armor. Putting on God's armor enables us to survive dark days and wicked individuals sent against us by the enemy. Wearing all of God's armor is a way of life and important to us. It describes preparation for battle against spiritual forces of darkness in a servant's daily walk and empowers us with an arsenal as we face storms, battles, struggles, and trouble that come with simply being a human being.

Ephesians 6:14-18, "*Stand therefore, having your loins girt about with truth, and having on the breastplate of righteousness; And your feet shod with the preparation of the gospel of peace; Above all, taking the shield of faith, wherewith ye shall be able to quench all the fiery darts of the wicked.* And take the helmet of salvation, and the sword of the Spirit, which is the word of God:

To have your loins girt with truth is having complete faith in God's truth and power to achieve the triumph. The breastplate of righteousness represents a true connection with God and His character in us. When our feet are shod with preparations for the gospel of peace, we are prepared to defeat the enemy and proclaim the gospel boldly.

The Helmet of Salvation constantly renews our ideals and belief in Him. The Sword of the Spirit represents God's Word, which we use as an offensive weapon against the adversary. But, more crucially, a faith in the reality of His Word and its magnificent conclusion. We are continually praying with all petitions and requests in sincerity while maintaining watch with persistence and appeals for all God's people.

The Shield of Faith is choosing faith over fear and enabling our faith to grow inside us not being shaken by trouble and challenges. As God freed the children of Israel from Egypt He performed many miracles, and one of the reasons for the miracles was to introduce Himself to them and to build their faith. When we look at the armour of God, we need the shield of faith in order to produce what the other parts of the armour. Principalities seek our faith most of all. Without faith, our lives and our salvation are jeopardized. All other armor parts require us to walk in our faith in God. The enemy uses all his weapons to attempt to make us question God and destroy our belief. He uses our troubles, struggles, traumas, difficulties, tests, temptations, and chastisements to decrease our faith. However, it is God who uses these same things to build our faith, supporting and guiding us. The choice as to which path to take is ours. We get to choose whether or not our faith is challenged daily. We believe our limited reasoning or God's evidence of His presence in our lives. If we lack belief in God, it is impossible to please or draw close to Him. Of all human considerations and the pieces of the armour of God, belief in God is the most fundamental. Hebrews 11:6 says, "But without faith, it is impossible to please him: for he that cometh to God must believe that he is and that he is a rewarder of them that diligently seek him. We are prone to disbelief by our own temptations, and the enemy causes us to twist the Word of God and mix it with lies and falsehoods to cause disbelief. It is often the trauma we experience in childhood or in various relationships that the enemy uses to twist our thoughts and actions and put us on the wrong fork in the road. The traumas we experience cause us unforgiveness, prevent us from letting go, and twist our thoughts and actions, causing us to walk outside of God's commandments, prevent us from growing in the fruit of the spirit, and prevent us from believing in God. The traumas, trials, and troubles are meant to increase our faith and cause us to believe God more and more. They are used to strengthen us and sanctify us, but Satan attempts to use them to cause disbelief. All we have to do is choose the right fork in the road to salvation. Just believe. Think like you believe, speak like you believe, walk as if you believe, and grow intentionally as if you believe because the stakes are high. The biggest stake is your salvation.

Ephesians 6:18, *Praying always with all prayer and supplication in the Spirit, and watching thereunto with all perseverance and supplication for all saints;*

Praying is always the last piece of armor. Many of us are seeking to understand the battles we face with a spiritual eye. We constantly attempt to analyze the spiritual warfare and the motives of principalities. With all prayer and supplication in the Spirit, we watch everything around us with all perseverance and supplication as saints and servants of God.

Being in the spirit is being in Christ as he is in the Father, being in both the Son and the Father is being in close fellowship with the two members of the Godhead, the 16th chapter of John explains it further. Prayer is essential for joining the ranks of biblically powerful people. It helps us become more like Christ and exposes the Father's heart and thinking to us so we can walk like him.

The Fruits of the Spirit

The "Fruits of the Spirit" lists characteristics and character traits in the Galatians passage below. The Apostle Paul refers to these traits as characteristics that we should exhibit in their life and are created by the Holy Spirit inside them. The Fruit of the Spirit are frequently regarded as crucial to living the life of a servant of God. We can employ the term "fruit" in a sentence like the "fruit of our labor" to express the outcomes of our efforts. Even if we don't harvest strawberries or apples, we can still have "fruit," a salary, a completed project, or even a child. According to the Apostle Paul, the "Fruit of the Spirit" develop from genuine repentance and transformation, a turning away from our sinful ways and toward love for God and others.

Galatians 5:22-23, "But the fruit of the Spirit is love, joy, peace, long-suffering, gentleness, goodness, faith, Meekness, temperance: against such there is no law." All the fruit of the spirit are important, but this study will only include a study of love, joy, peace, and faith, the foundation for all others.

The Fruit of Love

Love, particularly 'Agape love,' is often seen as the fundamental virtue and the greatest of all. This love, which comes from the Greek word ἀγάπη (Agape), is not just a human emotion but a divine gift. Greek has several terms for love, including eros (marital love) and Philos (brotherly love), but Agape is the ideal love that only God can provide. In terms of Agape, as used by God, it expresses a perfect Being's deep and constant 'love' and interest in entirely unworthy objects, producing and fostering a respectful 'love' in them towards the giver and a practical 'love' towards those who benefit from it, as well as a desire to assist others in seeking the Creator. Love for God and others stems from receiving God's complete agape love. Jesus, through his teachings and actions, demonstrated the practical application of Agape love. **1 John 4:7**, 'Beloved, let us love one another: for love is of God; and every one that loveth is born of God, and knoweth God.' Agape love is a selfless love that unifies and heals. We see God's love through the crucifixion of Jesus Christ. This love redeems and cures humanity amid sin and death. Agape translates to the Hebrew word for love, ahabah or ahavah, in many Old Testament scriptures such as in **Song of Solomon 2:4** "He brought me to the banqueting house, and his banner over me was love," It traces to **Deuteronomy 7:8**, "But because the Lord loved you, and because he would keep the oath which he had sworn unto your fathers, hath the Lord brought you out with a mighty hand, and redeemed you out of the house of bondmen, from the hand of Pharaoh king of Egypt."

The Fruit of Joy

Joy is the second fruit of the Spirit. The Hebrew transliteration for joy is 'simcha' according to Strong's Dictionary and it is not reliant on circumstances, but rather a profound sense of happiness and gladness that stems from a connection with God. Merriam-Webster defines 'joy' as "the emotion evoked by well-being, success, or good fortune or the prospect of possessing what one desires...the expression or exhibition of such emotion...a state of happiness." It is frequently observed in the Bible with an elevated state of happiness. It is the manifestation of God's favor and grace in one's life. Biblical pleasure is happiness that does not depend on our circumstances. **James 1:2** encourages, "My brethren, count it all **joy** when ye fall into divers' temptations." We know that the testing of our faith is what produces perseverance. The joy in **James 1:2** traces back to the Strong's Lexicon, Hebrew word "simcha" meaning exceedingly, gladness, pleasure and rejoicing. It is the base word for "sameach" and it means gladness of heart. **Jeremiah 33:11**, "The voice of joy, and the voice of gladness, the voice of the bridegroom, and the voice of the bride." According to Strong's this joy is the same type of gladness as in **Nehemiah 8:17**, "And all the congregation of them that were come again out of the captivity made booths, and sat under the booths: for since the days of Jeshua the son of Nun unto that day had not the children of Israel done so. And there was very great gladness."

When we really walk in God, actively trusting that he can and will deliver us from the challenges of life, we feel Joy, not sadness, because we remember he delivered us before, and we trust him. **Psalms 34:18** says, "The LORD is nigh unto them that are of a broken heart, and saveth such as be of a contrite spirit." Simcha is not just a feeling, it's an energy that invigorates us, propelling us forward in our faith. Simcha is not just a feeling, it's a transformative force that propels us forward, fostering growth and development. Its absence is what defines depression—no movement, no growth, no purpose, and no meaning. Life without Simcha is routine and mechanical; it is restricted, stale, and boring. **1 Peter 5:7**, "Casting all your care upon him; for he careth for you." If you are struggling with anything, your pathway is singing and reading psalms. Do something different. Celebrate God for resolving your problems yesterday, last month, and last year. Rejoice in the joy of His past resolutions, for they are a testament to His faithfulness. **James 5:13** says, "Is any among you afflicted? Let him pray. Is any merry? Let him sing psalms."

The more faith one gains, the more joy can fill our heart because we know that God can do all things. Joy from faith allows us to wear the shield of faith in a proactive way to help protect ourselves from negative energy and spiritual attacks. protect yourself from negative thoughts and feelings. Joy is not the icing on the cake but an essential ingredient in a complex batter in the cake with which we are to armor ourselves daily. In our most painful challenges, our losses and sufferings, we discover how deep the sweetness of being a servant of God is. The comfort and strength we find in our faith, is the essence in which such joy flows. Even through difficulty and darkness, joy is not thin, frivolous, and empty but thick, substantive, and complete. The reason is that after overcoming the storms of life, joy comes in the morning and that joy can be deeply sweet. Joy keeps us hopeful.

The Fruit of Peace

Peace promotes reconciliation with God and living in peace with others. Peace encompasses conflict-free living and harmony with God and others. Peace as in the following verses, eirene (in Greek), traces back to various Old Testament scriptures in Modern Hebrew such as əl¶wmî or the transliteration shalom, also shalowam in Paleo Hebrew which means peace, completeness, soundness, and welfare. **Romans 8:6**, "For to be carnally minded is death; but to be spiritually minded is life and peace."

A peaceful existence ensures physical and emotional safety. Peace comes from allowing the Holy Spirit to work in our hearts and brains. Peace traces other scriptures in such as **Isaiah 59:8** "The way of peace they know not; and there is no judgment in their goings: they have made them crooked paths: whosoever goeth therein shall not know peace." **John 14:27,** "Peace I leave with you, my peace I give unto you, not as the world giveth, give I unto you: let not your heart bee troubled, neither let it be afraid." As you consider what peace is, keep in mind that it is not the same as what the outside world provides. **John 16:33,** "These things I have spoken unto you, that in me ye might have peace. In the world ye shall have tribulation: but be of good cheer; I have overcome the world." Peace can be evoked by a variety of things, but it can only be fully experienced by the Spirit of God. tranquility, but the only authentic source of peace for an individual is the Spirit of God because of their faith.

The Fruit of Faith

Faith frees us from anxiety and worry about our finances, safety, salvation, and everlasting existence. Faith as a fruit of the spirit that is also part of the armour of God. **Ephesians 6:16,** "Above all, taking the shield of faith, wherewith ye shall be able to quench all the fiery darts of the wicked." The fruit of faith is visible in the serenity that overtake you even when your circumstances are far from calm when we overcome the adversity of the storms. One must have faith in order to "call on the name of the Lord." According to **Romans 10:14-21,** Israel still disobeyed even after hearing and comprehending the good news of the gospel. Paul demonstrated where and how Israel rejected the truth that God gave them by working through a number of questions. Paul made a very clear point. After receiving more than enough information, the Israelites had not acknowledged the Messiah. God continued to extend His hands to His people in spite of the failure and inconsistency of the faith. **Romans 10:14,** "How then shall they call on him in whom they have not believed? and how shall they believe in him of whom they have not heard? and how shall they hear without a preacher?"

According to **Hebrew 11:1,** we must trust what God says, although it sometimes appears like God is not honoring His covenantal promises to His servants. "Now faith is the substance of things hoped for, the evidence of things not seen. For by it the elders obtained a good report." **Hebrews 11:1-2**. A report must be heard, or received, in order to be considered. This emphasizes how crucial it is to be open to the message and to keep our hearts and brains open to believe in God, His promises, and His laws, statues, and judgements. The book of Hebrews is meant to challenge, encourage, and empower believers. According to this letter, Jesus Christ is superior to all other prophets and all other claims to truth. Since God has given us Christ, we should listen to what He says and not move backward. This is a crucial point that Hebrews emphasizes, as the consequences of ignoring God are dire. The book of Hebrews is essential for drawing on many portions of the Old Testament in making a case that Christ is the ultimate and perfect expression of God's plan for humanity. It presents some tough ideas about the faith of a servant of God, a fact the author makes specific note of.

The Hebrew word for faith is "emunah". Faith is an ongoing pursuit. Think of 'emunah,' or faith, as being similar to exercising to stay physically well. The spirit needs constant care to maintain its faith, just as a regular workout regimen is necessary for a healthy body. Faith is therefore an active verb, a lively endeavor and process that necessitates continuous and steadfast nurturing for growth, rather than a static noun, something one owns and never loses. As you reflect on the essence of faith, recognize that the fruit of faith carries a deeper meaning that implies not only belief but a deep commitment. "And these all, having obtained a good report through faith, received not the promise: God having provided some better thing for us, that they without us should not be made perfect." **Hebrew 11: 39-40**. Take time to remember God's promises, which means reading the word of God. When storms rage, try to impact your heart and find ease from the storms with reminders of God's goodness over your circumstances. It is the peace found in the midst of your faith that will keep you standing, unwavering and confident in God. We need God's armour to grow in the fruit of His spirit, and faith is a significant part of both.

JUST BELIEVE

Four things to believe that will improve the quality of your life so you can step into your power:

1. Believe it is possible to do anything God commands. Stop saying "I can't. It is too hard." God said all things are possible through Christ who strengthens you. Believe it!

2. Believe that everything God asked you to do is for your benefit. For example, he told us to forgive others. Hating your enemies is not for our own good. Forgiving adds power to our lives. Understand your own mistakes, repent, and forgive others so you can be forgiven.

3. Believe that God can change anyone. Pray for your enemies. You are not praying for them to get a new car or a new house or job. You are praying for their wellbeing for them to change and be a better person. When you pray for your enemies, he deals with them in a way that they will need to self-reflect in order for God to work with them. He will bring their sin and the hurt they caused you to their minds and unless they repent, it will torment them for a time, teaching them the lessons they need to learn in their lives. God may or may not bring to the apologize to you, but be okay with either. Hopefully, God will do something good in them and they will change so they will hurt no one else. Pray for them then move on and let God do his work. Praying for them will help you let it go.

4. Believe any circumstance will change in your life. Believe that God can take any affliction you experience and any mistake you have made around to your benefit. Many are the afflictions of the righteous but The Lord will deliver them out of them all. Believe your time is in God's hands, trust him.

5. Believe that if you are obedient, God promises that Nothing can separate us from the love of Christ. **Romans 8:35**. "Who shall separate us from the love of Christ? shall tribulation, or distress, or persecution, or famine, or nakedness, or peril, or sword?" Even when the world is spinning out of control, with despair and tragedy all around, we are securely held in the unbreakable grip of God's love because of our obedience.

You will find a list of God's promises in chapter 8, Useful Tools.

The Fruit of Patience

Patience is being slow to anger and demonstrating tolerance and patient with others, especially in difficult situations. Forbearance (makrothumia) is not a regularly used term. The Greek term in the Galatians passage is commonly translated as patience, endurance, constancy, steadfastness, persistence, long-suffering, and slowness in avenging wrongs. The Holy Spirit gives us the strength and endurance they need to face difficult circumstances. This word's Greek origin corresponds to two terms meaning "long" and "passion." We may bear temptation, thanks to the Holy Spirit and become "long-tempered" rather than "short-tempered." Paul used this term to describe Jesus' patience with him. **1 Timothy 1:16,** "Howbeit for this cause I obtained mercy, that in me first Jesus Christ might shew forth all long-suffering, for a pattern to them which should hereafter believe on him to life everlasting." Like Paul, we have all profited from Christ's incredible patience with us. The Holy Spirit's presence in our lives is also demonstrated by our capacity to persist, be patient, steady, and long-tempered. **Ephesians 4:1,** "I therefore, the prisoner of the Lord, beseech you that ye walk worthy of the vocation wherewith ye are called." Patience does not equate to passive permissiveness but active perseverance. **James 1:4** "But let patience have her perfect work, that ye may be perfect and entire, wanting nothing." An idea discussed in the book of James is suffering. When confronted with life situations challenging their faith, James urges servants to consider it pure joy. The reason is that they know that hardships brought on by their faith result in endurance, they can look upon their sufferings with delight. Endurance, a key player in our spiritual growth, has a clear end goal: perfection, completeness, wholeness. It's not the suffering that leads to maturity, but our active endurance as we suffer through challenges and strugglers. As believers, we are called to 'let patience have its perfect work,' emphasizing the importance of our response. Even in the face of trials, our consistent endurance in life is what fosters Christian maturity, not just the suffering we endure. Read the entire first chapter of James. Be sure to pray for understanding.

Remember how God introduced himself to Moses and the children of Israel. He performed miracles so they could be freed from bondage in Egypt. Imagine if they could have focused on the beauty of God and the power he showed them when he performed those miracles. Imagine if they would have remembered those miracles as they experienced challenges in the wilderness. Imagine how different their outcome would have been if they could have remembered the joy of the Lord they felt when he parted the Red Sea and praised him for performing such a miracle on their behalf each time they needed water as they traveled, each time they needed food and each time they faced an enemy. Imagine if they had focused on the miracle after miracle he performed for them to keep them safe as they traveled and used praise to boost their confidence in him each time they feared.

Reread their story, starting in Exodus, and then reread **Psalm 78**. Remember that God is able. Now, learn from their mistakes, praise God, pray to him, and meditate on his Word when things go wrong instead of existing in worry, fear, doubt, and anxiety. Remember the things, situations, and people he has delivered you from. Write them down in your journal and reread the list when you doubt. Use your examples and the experiences of the children of Israel to deliberately change your mindset in order for you to navigate trouble and push forward. These lessons are not just historical accounts, but they are tools for your personal growth and spiritual development.

Let these be lessons in perseverance instead of reasons to quit. Let these lessons help you practice the fruits of the spirit. See failure and setbacks as lessons instead of looking at them as permanent. Mental reformation does not happen overnight but over time. Let those lessons light up your brain, thus brightening your energy so that you attract contagious solutions, goodness, and positivity that influence others. Your thoughts shape your actions, and your actions change your outcomes. Unlock your greatness by changing how you think, and don't be paralyzed by negative and limited thoughts and beliefs. Think of doubt as a belief. Think of fear as a means of paralysis. Think of depression as limited thinking. Think of sadness as a tool of the enemy causing you to live in the past, whether yesterday, last week, last year, last month or the last decade.

This thinking limits your courage to progress and move forward in personal development, career, life's goals, or spirituality. Stop that now! **Psalm 31:24**, "Be of good courage, and he shall strengthen your heart, all ye that hope in the Lord." The courage comes from having a conference with God because He's omnipresent, omniscient, and omnipotent. To confirm it, we have to know him, and in order to know it, we have to read God's Word.

Step into the power of God because this is where your power lies. Let these lessons help the Word of God be your tool to unlock God's power,

and you step in it by allowing it to change the framework through which you see your challenges. Let it reframe your mindset, your vision, and your purpose. Remember, it is not just your own strength that you rely on, but the infinite power of God that can transform your life.

The children of Israel held the key to getting to the new land. Nevertheless, they didn't know how to use that key. But you do when you examine their mistakes and apply them to your life, and you think. Their outcome was the result of their decisions, and so was yours. Do not be your saboteur. Step into your power. Learn, self-reflect, and grow; take the necessary steps to evolve and pray about it. Do what they couldn't do, and learn from what they didn't do right.

Don't just put in the armor; use them. Don't just be aware of the fruit of the spirit, embrace them with intentionality. The fruit of the spirit and the armor of God can help you make the transformations you need to determine the trajectory of your life, and an added bonus is you step into the power of eternal salivation as you become focused on not only the law but the weightier matters. The armor and the fruit are directly connected to how you love God with all your heart, soul, and might as is suggested in **Matthew 22:37, Mark 12:20**, and **Luke 10:27**. We were first told in **Deuteronomy 6:5**, "And thou shalt love the LORD thy God with all thine heart, and with all thy soul, and with all thy might."

Ensure Continuous Growth

Identify personal hurt or trauma. Anxiety tells us to avoid the issues, but do not avoid it. Once you feel the discomfort, pray, praise, and meditate instead. Stretch your comfort zone. Do not believe the voice in your head that tells you to evade it. Push past it with a therapist, a friend, or prayer and praise. If you avoid the things that make you anxious you cannot push past it.

Acknowledge hurtful emotions if the door is open let people know what they did to cause you harm. If they are servants of God embarking on continuous growth they may ask what they can do to restore the harm. Be ready for a situation or a person who does not ask or care to restore harm done to you. Stimulants reduces healthy brain activity. They supercharge your anxious thoughts. Do not fuel your anxious thoughts so that thoughts of doom and gloom are heightened. Try physical exercise instead. Try pray and praise to better manage your anxiety.

Know that when you are sitting in sadness, stress, and anxiety, your brain creates more doom and gloom, more anger, and more hatred. It is like unto a child who has nothing to do, they create all kinds of things to do that is not necessarily good things. Think of the old adage, "an idle mind is a devil's workshop." Engage your sad and depressed mind a project you can enjoy or one you need.

Nutrition, health, and wellness is important when you have negative emotions. Do not skip meals. Do not eat carbohydrates like chips and fries that do not nourish your brain. Eat 6 small meals each day. Eat a healthy breakfast, lunch, and dinner. Focus on caloric energy; brain fuel. When your brain runs out of energy your emotional regulation, stress tolerance, and social toleration will suffer. Alternately, if you are not eating anyway because of your anxiety, turn it into an intentional fast and prayer.

Stop trying to do everything yourself. Stop thinking you can handle the stress and depression by yourself. Everyone needs community. Build your community with people with whom you can fellowship and be social. Find an exercise partner. Find a study partner. Find someone to watch a movie with you. Share your feelings with someone who love you or make an appoint with a therapist. You need someone to talk to and do not be reluctant to delegate and ask for help.

Understand that you are human and you make mistakes. Do not treat yourself like an unreliable person. You made a mistake, so what, learn from it and move on. Forgiving yourself.

Forgive others. You may not want to forgive, but you have to forgive them anyway. You do not however have to put yourself in the position to be harmed by that person who hurt you and caused you harm. Forgiveness is not for the person who harmed you but for you. Let go. Let God witness your forgiveness.

How To Let Go

What is the process for letting go?

1. Focus on the breath. Take deep breaths.
2. Breathe in compassion for your mistakes and others mistakes. Breath in
3. Meditate on the Word.
4. Forgive and forgive often. Do not hold on to stuff.
5. Pray for the person who caused you harm.
6. Develop an attitude of gratitude. Be grateful for things that are NOT wrong.
7. Be grateful for your new positive thoughts and actions.
8. Let yourself feel love, so you can act in loving manner.

A Way to Draw Close to God

There are few things better than spending time with family and close friends. Taking time for the people in our lives helps build our connections and makes them develop stronger. Your relationship with God is no different. He made us so that He might draw close to us as we spend time drawing close to Him. Prayer coupled with meditation are ways to get that done.

Growing in the fruit of the spirit requires more than just passive reading; it involves active learning and constant reflection. Writing regular gratitude journal entries can help to draw you closer to God. Some call this type of writing devotionals. Use them to teach yourself how to pray and what to pay. Be sure to choose a quiet comfortable place that encourages quiet, peace, and tranquility.

Choose the fruit of the spirit in which you need to grow. Think about why. Write it down. Think of specific examples that helped you make this decision. Neuroscientist, Dr. Caroline Leaf in her book, Who Switched Off My Brain? Controlling Toxic Thoughts and Emotion stated, if you pray 12 minutes a day your brain is impacted. When it is done consistently and is focused, over a period of 8 weeks, there is a physical advantage. You are on the road to change the structure of your brain causing you to create good energy, increasing your ability to have more joy and allowing you to more positive days, reducing your depression and anxiety. Prayer and meditating also changes the structure of your brain enough for it to be measured on a brain scan. Prayer and meditating on the Word breaks negative cycles that keeps a person sad, fearful, critical, and unforgiving. What might happen when you are consistent and move beyond 12 minutes and 8 weeks?

Begin to meditate. The focus of meditation is not about thinking. It's not even about relaxing. It is about brain work. You are training your brain, restructuring it so that it transforms itself, ridding the amygdala part of your brain of any darkness. Darkness cannot live where there is light. Your brain won't multi-task. You're lighting up your brain. Worry, fear, sadness, or any negative thought or emotion cannot dwell in the amygdala together. Your thoughts focus on either positive or negative thoughts, one or the other, not both. This tells me to do whatever I need to do in order to change my thoughts from positive to negative.

TAKE A MEDITATION BREAK

1. Put your pen down. Rest your hands in your lap. Choose a comfortable position.
2. Soften your gaze, lower or close your eyes, prepare to focus your attention on the passage you chose for this gratitude journal.
3. Begin by taking two or three full, deep breaths. Breathing out of your mouth. Feel your body release anxiousness, pressure or tension as you exhale. Now, gently close your lips and begin breathing at a natural pace through your nose.
4. Bring your attention to the sensation of air moving into and out of your body. On the inhale, notice it traveling into your nose, your throat, down into your lungs. Notice the rise in your chest and belly. On the exhale, notice how the air leaves your body.
5. Continue like this for two minutes. Noticing the breath moving into your body on the inhale, and leaving your body on the exhale.
6. Now, focus your attention on the bible passage you chose for this gratitude journal.
7. When your mind wanders, gently guide it back to your breath and focus your attention on the passage you chose for this gratitude journal. Our passage. Don't judge yourself, wandering

for a moment is no big deal. Just bring it back to the breath and to your passage.

8. Meditate as long as you want, let your body decide for you. When you're done, calmly expand your attention back to your surroundings then back to your journaling.

Negative vs Positive Self-Talk

It's a profound struggle to see ourselves clearly when dealing with negative self-talk. This self-talk, often influenced by harsh remarks and challenging situations, significantly shapes our daily lives. When I say 'clearly,' I mean seeing ourselves truthfully. The lens through which we view ourselves is a powerful force that significantly influences how we live in every moment of every day. Negative self-talk can create a personal hell. A personal hell could be a never-ending cycle, and we often create the never-ending hell ourselves through our thoughts, our choices and negative self-talk. Your fear, insecurities, and trauma create the stories which increases the personal hell. Do what you need to do to control your thoughts because your thoughts impact your attitude and your attitude impacts?

Your personal journey of moderation, emotional restraint, restraint from excess, discretion, willpower, and self-control are of utmost importance. It's the key to your success and personal growth, allowing you to avoid temptations and achieve your goals. The ability to delay gratification and resist unwanted behaviors, and unrighteous and negative urges are increased by positive self-talk. Temperance is also the ability to control your thoughts and worries. It's a crucial starting point for our discussion on temperance. **Galatians 5: 22-23** talks about the fruits of the spirit, and the one we talk little about is temperance and how to accomplish that level of self-control and restraint.

1. What is the specific matter that is causing me stress and anxiety?
2. Am I letting matters that are out of my control stress me out?
3. How is this a matter of self-control and an opportunity to grow in temperance?

Be aware of negative self-talk. Stop speaking defeat in your life. Unchecked, the bulk of your self-talk may poison your outlook on your present situation, weaken your soul, and deplete your vitality. Recognize that if left unchecked, the negative storyteller in your mind may destroy your faith, exaggerate your anxieties, and instill sentiments of hopelessness and self-sabotage. Negative self-talk is your inner voice making critical, harmful, or punitive statements. These are the negative, mean-spirited, or unjustly critical thoughts that arise when you make judgments about yourself. Everyone has an inner critic. At times, this tiny voice can be a source of guidance, keeping us motivated toward our objectives, such as when it tells us that what we're going to consume isn't healthy or that what we're about to do is risky. Do not allow your negative self-talk to create an environment that destroys you, your success, and the people around you. Think of your words as a tool. They start with a thought and build into battles that you did not need to fight.

Negative self-talk can take many forms. It can sound like this:

- "I'm not good at this, so I should avoid attempting it for my own personal safety."
- "I can never do anything right!"
- "I don't deserve to be happy!"
- "I'll fail anyways, so what's the point of trying."
- "That looks really hard. Even if I tried, I'd never be able to do it."
- "I got a C on this test. I guess I'm not good at math."
- "I'll never be able to go to a good college."
- "Nothing every goes my way."
- "I have so much bad luck.".
- "Sometimes, I wish I had never been born."

The examples of negative self-talk above may seem like a realistic appraisal of a situation. only to devolve into a fear-based fantasy and stories created in your head. Negative self-talk is not only unpleasant and stressful, but it may also create difficulty to stay motivated to attain your objectives, achieve your goals and increase your spiritual growth.

Your inner critic's thoughts may sound similar to those of a critical parent or friend from the past. It may exhibit common cognitive biases such as catastrophizing and blaming. However, it's important to remember that negative self-talk is not a permanent state. It is defined as any inner conversation you have with yourself that may impede your capacity to believe in yourself and your skills and realize your full potential. With awareness and effort, you can overcome it and create positive changes in your life and your belief in your abilities. This voice can often prove more destructive than beneficial, especially when it becomes overly negative. Negative self-talk may be quite depressing. Most of us encounter negative self-talk at some point in our lives, and it may take numerous forms. It also causes enormous stress, not only for us but also for people around us, if we are not mindful. This is what you need to know about negative self-talk and how it affects your body, mind, life, and relationships. One negative thought turns into another negative thought and they snowball. "For as he thinketh in his heart, so is he, **"Proverbs 23:7"**.

Negative self-talk occurs when you compare yourself to others. When you gaze at someone else's life and feel that yours isn't as distinctive, satisfying, fantastic, or joyful; this occurs when you criticize yourself. When you indulge in self-judgment and make harsh and unjustified assessments of your value, it is the harm done when blaming yourself. Complaining also promotes negative self-talk and when you focus too much on the bad aspects of a situation in your life in general rather than acting to change it. On the other hand, positive self-talk involves affirming statements like 'I am capable ', 'I am worthy ', 'I can overcome this challenge '. It is therapeutic and transforming, just as negative self-talk is destructive and toxic.

If you are in the habit of putting yourself down, building self-esteem begins by learning how to talk to yourself. Begin by making a list of all that you have accomplished so far in your life. Everything from your past such as graduating with honors or making the track team in high school, to juggling work and family, to being able, to baking cookies from scratch, belongs on your accomplishments list. List the things you do well today and how you have grown in capacity, skill, intellect, and attitude. Add to this list whenever you think of anything at all in your life you should be proud of. Refer to this list often when your confidence needs a boost and keep adding to it. It is critical to silence and remove the automatic negative thoughts that might derail your life if allowed to. Learn to love yourself fully and openheartedly. The world is in sync with your individuality and ready for your next move. It's important to celebrate your victories in life, no matter how small. Concentrate on the good and what you can accomplish right now. Be grateful for all you have, including the gift of life. Gratitude alone indicates that your life has a purpose.

Negative self-talk is a habit that has to be broken. Don't treat yourself like your worst enemy. You wouldn't let anyone else talk to you that way, so don't let YOU talk to you that way. Pay attention to your needs. Taking care of your own needs is one way of self-esteem building. Choosing healthy foods, exercising, allowing yourself adequate sleep and time to relax are all ways to show yourself that you are of value. You have something unique. Your strength is in the Word of God, and when you embrace it, you unlock the power inside you.

Samples of Positive Self-Talk

I can push through challenges because I trust God and I am confident that HE will direct me. Scripture for prayer & meditation Proverbs 3:5-6 "Trust in the LORD with all thine heart; and lean not unto thine own understanding. In all thy ways acknowledge him, and he shall direct thy paths."

Let HIM bless your day. I have faith that everything will work out for my best because God will uphold me and help me. Scripture for prayer and meditation Isaiah 41:10 "Fear thou not; for I am with thee: be not dismayed; for I am thy God: I will strengthen thee; yea, I will help thee; yea, I will uphold thee with the right hand of my righteousness."

I find peace in letting go of what was, I embrace what is and welcome what is to come. Scripture for prayer and meditation. **Exodus 14:14** "The LORD shall fight for you, and ye shall hold your peace."

I am renewed today as I shift my perspective so I can be a spiritual man (or woman) as I cope with difficulty and challenges. Scripture for prayer & meditation **2 Corinthians 4:16-18** "For which cause, we faint not; but though our outward man perish, yet the inward man is renewed day by day."

I am blessed. I am healed. I am confident. I am growing in the fruits of the spirit. I am able and grateful. I can do all things because Christ is my source of strength. Scripture for prayer & meditation: **Philippians 4:13** "

I can do all things through Christ which strengthened me." I keep hope in my heart, even on the toughest days. To free myself from depression and anxiety, I pray to God, who is my help, and meditate on his Word. Scripture for prayer and meditation: **Psalm 121:1-2**, "I will lift up mine eyes unto the hills, from whence cometh my help. My help cometh from the Lord, which made heaven and earth."

I am strong. **Ephesians 6:10**, "Finally, my brethren, be strong in the Lord, and in the power of his might."

I am enough. **2 Corinthians 3:5**, "Not that we are sufficient of ourselves to think any thing as of ourselves; but our sufficiency is of God;"

I am loved. **Romans 5:8**, "But God commendeth his love toward us, in that, while we were yet sinners, Christ died for us."

Have confidence in yourself because you have confidence in God. These are some scriptures that build my confidence in God, thus, myself. Find those that build your confidence in this way.

- Proverbs 28:128 The wicked flee when no man pursueth: but the righteous are bold as a lion.
- Proverbs 3:26 For the LORD shall be thy confidence, and shall keep thy foot from being taken.
- Isaiah 41:10 Fear thou not; for I am with thee: be not dismayed; for I am thy God: I will strengthen thee; yea, I will help thee; yea, I will uphold thee with the right hand of my righteousness.
- 2 Corinthians 3:5 Not that we are sufficient of ourselves to think any thing as of ourselves; but our sufficiency is of God;
- 1 John 3:20-21 For if our heart condemn us, God is greater than our heart, and knoweth all things. Beloved, if our heart condemn us not, then have we confidence toward God.
- Philippians 4:13 I can do all things through Christ which strengtheneth me.
- Hebrews 13:6 So that we may boldly say, The Lord is my helper, and I will not fear what man shall do unto me.
- Romans 15:13 Now the God of hope fill you with all joy and peace in believing, that ye may abound in hope, through the power of the Holy Ghost.

As your confidence develops your confidence will cause your feelings and mood to change. When your mood changes it will be like a magnet and the right people, the right opportunities, and the right resources will come to you. Then you can begin to build the beauty you need to accomplish your goals and to impact others in a positive way. Your energy will shift. People will begin to see the light of God in you. Without the confidence in God, you exude a darkness that pushes people away. This growing confidence in God will permeate your environment and you will feel a joy that will not come from anything man made.

4

Gratitude Journal

efore journaling, pray. Your gratitude journal can be used as daily devotionals. Open yourself up to pray a prayer of thankfulness God throughout your day. Invite Him to be a part of your journaling session, and ask Him to lead you where He wants you to go. Express at least five things you are grateful for.

As you whisper your prayer, write the fruit of the spirit you chose. Tell why you chose that fruit. Ask for help in your growth. Don't be afraid of how He will teach you, remember He knows you, you've already shown Him your love because you keep His commandments. His methods of teaching are good for your character and your growth.

LEAVE IT IN HIS HANDS

1. Choose a verse or section of verses to focus your writing and on which to meditate.
2. Read each verse three times, once silently, once out loud, and one more time silently.
3. Reflect on the words and say another prayer that you will be able to understand and properly convey His message through your writing.
4. Write without stopping to think about the words you're putting down. Let them flow as you share the message(s) you hear from

God about the scripture. You can (and should) go back and neaten things up, but at this point let God's words flow through you.

5. End by writing a finishing Prayer.

When you finish writing, pray again. Write the first part of this prayer as an end to your devotional. Then, keep praying. Thank God for calling you into his fold and letting you be His ambassador. Brighten your light. Ask that your words reach the deepest part of your soul and shine through you so you are a light to others and the fruit of the spirit grows in you.

Gratitude Journal Entries

#JEREMIAH9EXPERIENCE

Today, I am in complete control of my thoughts. I am blessed to have a family who loves me.

Create a Brain Blast

There is a difference between being a depressed person and being depressed. Yet either can be overcome by giving yourself a BRAIN BLAST using Biblical meditation, positive self-talk, and positive I am statements. A BRAIN BLAST is positive self-talk coupled with the Word of God that assists in breaking negative thought habits, recognizing strengths, cultivating mental clarity, trusting intuition, focusing on both the promises of God and the positive elements of life, and overcoming challenges. Positive self-talk works, as a BRAIN BLAST, but the key is the deep emotional connection that comes from sincerity and vulnerability.

You cannot expect monotonous, robotic affirmations to improve your life. They become insincere. You can't expect to benefit from repeating phrases that you don't believe in. Positive statements function when you think they are true. You may not feel them right away since there is usually an adjustment period, which can vary from person to person, in which you allow the notion of the affirmation to be true for you. Put your heart into it. Once you get into that feeling area, the affirmation will begin to reflect in your daily experience, especially when you include appropriate scriptures in your positive self-talk. Words may be quite powerful in creating a BRAIN BLAST, especially when used correctly, at the proper time, and coupled with encouraging scriptures.

To develop a BRAIN BLAST and your I am statements, begin by defining your goals, and then write a brief statement that captures the passion behind them. Make sure to write or talk to yourself in the present tense. Keep it brief and pleasant. Be specific. Include at least one emotion or feeling term in your message. The feelings are how you get to your amygdala which controls your emotions, memory, and decision making.

How to Create a BRAIN BLAST

1. Read the scripture passage,
2. Use it in your meditation.
3. Exercise the passage in your self-talk.
4. Pray the scripture: repeat it to God in your prayers, remind him what he said to you in his Word.
5. Pull down what he predetermined he'd do for his servants. (this means you have to read.)
6. Take a pause and reflect on gratitude and how great and capable God is. Know that all things are possible because He is powerful and when you show Him your love by being obedient to His word, He will respond favorably to your needs.
7. Implement prayer, meditation, and self-talk at least 3 times daily.
8. What other scriptures will you practice today?

Sister, See Yourself in the Literature

Read the following scriptures and picture yourself in them. See yourself as the amazing woman that God created. If you're like many women, you've likely felt like the Bible is not talking about you plenty of times. In truth, some bible teachers teach that God has no regard for women and women were created to submit to a husband. I disagree, from that perspective, because there are too many of examples whereby He showed love and regard for women in the Bible. In God's eyes, you're an amazing woman. In fact, seeing yourself the way God does is the key to living the way He wants you to live. Seek further revelations from God about the person He created. Discover your strengths. You may have a personal quality employed to serve others and advance God's purpose for your life. In one way the act of service will not only advance God's purpose but also bring you a sense of purpose and fulfillment.

Find your passion and purpose. Pray about it; it will make you feel fulfilled and happy. The act of prayer will reassure you and guide you in your journey. Seek further revelations from God about the person He created. Discover your strengths, talents, and particular methods to use your abilities to uplift others and advance God's kingdom. You may desire to serve others to advance God's purpose for your life. In one way, the act of service will not only advance God's purpose but also bring you a sense of purpose and fulfillment. Are you an organizer or do you have the ability to motivate others? Reflect on the relationships in your life, these could range from those with your closest friends and family to those with other people in your circle. Consider the kinds of individuals you might be most suited to help, consider those you are most attracted to and those you perform best around. Think about those you have the greatest sympathy for and those who seem to benefit from your distinctive abilities and skills. Use this book as a tool for self-reflection and step into your power where God is. In the process of partaking in the Jeremiah 9 Woman experience, you'll learn to embrace who you are so you can become all God created you to be.

"Man up" Through Your Storms

When the scriptures speak of "man" it is speaking to both male and females. The term "Man up" is typically used as a masculine term meaning to be tough, the phrase started in the military in around 1947 as a term meaning that each soldier was to go to their station assigned to them; their stations had to be "manned up" rather than "manned." Some communities have used the term to encourage boys and young men to act like men, to be strong to be tough. The term "Woman up" doesn't attract attention nor does it have the same impact of the term "Man up", Man is a species not a gender. We have male man and we are female man. So, in this respect, "man up" could apply to both men and women.

I'm taking the power to redefine "man up". This is my definition. "Man up" is the ability to be strong in the Lord, to trust in the power of his might. To understand that He has the power to change things and we need to "man up" and pray until something happens. God is our strength and He is our help when life gets to "life-ing". Our Father wants us to thrive and not just survive. We do not have to do it alone, He sent His only begotten son so we can lean on His son to give us hope and help. Then in John 10:27 Jesus said that His sheep hears His voice. However, to hear His voice, we have to study the word so we get to know Him, pray without fail, and learn to follow His lead and His direction. He is our hope and the path to hope is fully assured when we are right with God, when He knows we love Him by being obedient (John 14:15). This is part of the "Man up" process.

REFLECTING ON THE ROLE OF WOMEN

1. When the Word of God talks about saints, righteousness, and salvation, are these only related to men?
2. How do women come to be in these scriptures?
3. What do the prophets tell us about the debate over the role of women in the Old Testament?
4. At the time the New Testament was recorded, what were the early writers saying about the role of women?
5. What could and/or could not women do in the early church?
6. Should women work in the church? Why or why not?
7. Who were Jesus' female disciples?
8. What was their role?
9. What did Paul say about women who worked alongside him? Are the traditional customs severely critical, where ministry is for men only or did the custom derive from the Torah law?
10. What are the people saying about it now, in contemporary times?
11. Is there a difference between a leader of a church and a ministry?
12. Where do you stand on the issue of women in as prophetess, teachers, and disciples? Why? How is salvation communal?
13. How is salvation personal to men or women?
14. How can you as a woman experience our daily salvation walk with joy walking in His will and serving?

The Value of a Woman Who Prays and Studies

Why is it so vital for a woman to pray and study? Nearly 400 times the Bible says to pray. God not only commands us to pray, but He also provides us with models of effective prayer, prayers we can imitate, and even a formula for prayer that comes directly from Jesus in the Lord's prayer. **1 Thessalonians 5:15-18** is among the important scriptures telling us to pray constantly. "See that none render evil for evil unto any man; but ever follow that which is good, both among yourselves, and to all men. Rejoice evermore. Pray without ceasing. In everything give thanks: for this is the will of God in Christ Jesus concerning you."

Why should we pray? As we have often heard, "prayer changes things." As believers and followers of The Father and His Son, we ought to be inspired to engage with the Bible so that we might keep learning and developing what we have already learned and so that we may better our understanding of prayer to increase our faith. To better comprehend and implement the lessons found in the books of Scripture in our daily lives, we must expand our knowledge of their histories and social climate. It is important to get a deeper grasp of boundaries established and what is expected of us as women of God. **Jeremiah 9:17-20** is as important as **Proverbs 31:10-31**. These two passages convey to women what is expected of women. Studying helps us know better how to pray. As we saw earlier in the study of The Armour of God, prayer is the last piece of the armour of God. Praying opens the lines of communication with God. Study and prayer an interdependent They are critical since the adversary is constantly searching for openings. A woman who prays is crucial because she maintains the strength of that armor, even for those who might not be saved or may not pray as frequently.

I read the Bible in a different way after surrendering my life to God. My quiet time was a time to meet with God and get to know Him; it was no longer something I had to do. My confidence in Him grew as I got to know Him more; I thought He would act and respond. Studying strengthens my conviction that God alters everything when it comes to prayer. Studying also quiets the worry, doubt, and fear that tries to creep into my thoughts allowing me to focus on the business of praying for the situations that plague me and other believers and trust that God can and will deliver us. **1 Thessalonians 4:11** "And that ye study to be quiet, and to do your own business, and to work with your own hands, as we commanded you;" A woman of strength kneels in prayer and keeps her prayer muscle in shape, and ridding herself of fear from troubles and trauma.

There are many things that cause us fear. **2 Timothy 1:7** tells us not to fear. "For God hath not given us the spirit of fear; but of power, and of love, and of a sound mind." Prayer and study help us to tap into the power and love so we have a sound mind as we walk this walk. Without study and prayer, we are disquieted and uneasy allowing doubt to creep in. It is required of us to pray to keep the lines of communication open with God and to increase our faith. Despite the fact that God is aware of our needs before we even consider asking. Even while we have faith that God will provide for our necessities, we are still required to pray. Our purpose in praying is not to check with God, nor to remind Him, nor to prod Him. We pray in order to confess our complete reliance on the Lord and to honor His name. What occurs when a woman prays and sincerely thinks that God will hear her? If she keeps her eyes fastened on Him, she sees His response. He answers her and gives her peace while she waits. **Isaiah 26:3** "Thou wilt keep him in perfect peace, whose mind is stayed on thee: because he trusteth in thee."

5

Building a Personal Prayer Life

tart a gratitude journal. In your gratitude journal, list five to ten things you are thankful for daily. The activity facilitates the development of fresh ideas and neurological pathways that promote healing. A person's brain will unconsciously rewire to process negative information, primarily if they worry excessively about unfavorable outcomes. According to a neurology study, our minds are unable to simultaneously focus on positive and negative information. We may teach the brain to preferentially focus on positive emotions and thoughts by intentionally practicing thankfulness, which can lessen anxiety and depression.

If we are serious about character development and change as adults, we have to go through uncomfortable situations intentionally. We have to stop trying to dodge the process because it's the only way to grow. Change, however, can be rather painful. If we focus on the hurt, we will continue to suffer. If we focus on the lesson that comes from hurt, we will continue to grow. **Romans 12:2,** tells us not to copy the behavior and customs of this world, but let God transform us into a new person by changing the way we think. Then we will learn to know God's will for us, which is good and pleasing and perfect. "And be not conformed to this world: but be ye transformed by the renewing of your mind, that ye may prove what is that good, and acceptable, and perfect, will of God." When we change how we think, we change how we act, then our character is developed.

This is more of a personal reflection and testimony. When I was a teen and young adult going through stuff my daddy used to always ask "what did you learn?" I hated that question but it taught me how to learn from my mistakes, thus building my character. I have learned to appreciate and value the question over the years. I found that some things were out of my control and in the hands of God and maybe society. The Lord caused me to bring the scripture to life for myself and apply it to my life, developing my character. **Philippians 4:6** "Be careful for nothing; but in everything by prayer and supplication with thanksgiving let your requests be made known unto God." Whereas, the things that I can control are my attitude, how I perceive things, and respond to them, my level of resilience, my emotional well-being, and how I react to challenges I face.

Through the process of reflection and journaling, I learned to keep the question my father asked in mind, I learned what **Philippians 4:8-9**, meant and how to use it. "Finally, brethren, whatsoever things are true, whatsoever things are honest, whatsoever things are just, whatsoever things are pure, whatsoever things are lovely, whatsoever things are of good report; if there be any virtue, and if there be any praise, think on these things." There was honor and justice in what my struggles taught and because of my father's questions, I learned to allow the lessons I learned in my troubles to bring me peace. Believe me it was not easy but after much bellyaching and feelings of worry in the pit of my stomach, and even many days of teary eyes, I am getting better and better at it, yet I have not found my struggles lovely yet. Honestly, I may not ever get to that point. I can look back and see my struggles as builders of my character and improving the virtue in me. The good report is that I believe without the struggles. I would not be on the path to righteousness I am on now. I do not believe I would have become a woman who prays and grows in faith as deeply had it not been for the reflective questions my father asked me after a mistake.

Consequently, without learning to pray through my struggles I could have easily turned and returned back to the world where some people appear to live good lives, for the time at least. Today I am thinking about my challenges and how my gratitude for the things that were NOT wrong continues to help me change and grow in both character and belief. What I have learned and received and heard and seen in challenges, I have learned to give to God and leave it with him. Prayer, praise, and meditation were my tools to help me practice doing that. Therefore, the God of peace is with me WHEN I accomplish this goal. There are no fixed ways to grow in those areas. I do know that **Ephesians 4:22-24** helped me in this process. "That ye put off concerning the former conversation the old man, which is corrupt according to the deceitful lusts; And be renewed in the spirit of your mind; And that ye put on the new man, which after God is created in righteousness and true holiness." I am sure each person in this group can offer suggestions that work. Changing and growing is a matter of deciding the process which best suits us and taking necessary actions to walk on that path, understanding that the process can even change at any juncture. **Ephesians 4:23**, suggests we let the spirit of God renew our thoughts and attitudes. "And be renewed in the spirit of your mind;" When I used my father's question to guide the way I thought about my struggles, challenges, and troubles then combined it with prayer, meditation, showing gratitude, and praising God, I saw changes in myself. As I continue in this process, I am able to continue the growth process, although admittedly, sometimes it is still painful. Working through the pain is a benefit to my salvation. I have heard some say, salvation is not personal but it is common. Yes, I believe it is common too, but I have learned that striving for it makes salvation very personal.

A personal reflection requires us to think about the process of changing our mindsets and functioning within those things we can control. Changing our lives for the better is about us, the details of our desires, our specific environment, our goals and aspirations, and our motivation to continue to strive for a fulfilled, healthy, and righteous life. Life is a journey, and one way to change our lives for the better is to accept that there are many things about life that are out of our control, those we give to God. But the ones in our control we pray and work to change them. What I have learned is that God will help us with that process as well. Remember, we can do anything we set our minds to do because **Matthew 19:26** says "with God all things are possible. I saw this phrase on my timeline one week and thought it prompted a deep and serious reflection. "GROW through what you GO through!"

Self-Reflection: What does this mean to you? What have you gone through that you have grown through? What have you learned that God has helped you through? What were the valuable lessons in the journey?

Gratitude Will Help You Step Into Your Power

Gratitude is a pleasant feeling brought about by thankfulness and appreciation, and it has been linked to a variety of mental and physical health advantages, especially for pushing through depression and anxiety. When you are grateful, you express your appreciation for something or someone in your life by being kind, pleasant, and amiable. The word gratitude can have a variety of connotations depending on who uses it and in what context. Gratitude is the recognition that something good has happened to you. It also entails accepting responsibility for whatever small or big thing for which you are grateful. Feelings of gratitude frequently arise naturally in the present and is often short lived and temporary. Neurologists suggests that intentionally nurturing such thankfulness and allowing it to be a bit longer lasting can have mental health advantages.

Gratitude, in my experience, indicates a robust anti-anxiety technique. Its benefits surpass the potential to support relationships, enhance mental health, and alleviate stress. Scientists suggest that the effects of gratitude could be long-lasting and remarkably beneficial. Numerous studies have demonstrated that gratitude is a cost-free, uncomplicated, and potential strategy to combat anxiety because the amygdala cannot think about gratitude and anxiety at the same time. Anxiety is a common experience, one that affects almost everyone. "The American Psychological Association defines anxiety as an emotion characterized by feelings of tension, worried thoughts, and physical changes like increased blood pressure." The fact that gratitude interventions are cost-free and straightforward empowers us to manage our anxiety effectively.

What exactly does anxiety feel like? Anxiety manifests itself in a variety of ways, including feelings of nervousness, restlessness, and tension.

When you are anxious, you may feel a sense of approaching danger, fear, catastrophe, or sorrow. Symptoms of depression and anxiety include difficulty sleeping and stomach issues. Anxiety is a physiological response to stress, emotional hurt, or pain. Some stress is normal, and learning to cope with it is an important part of maintaining a healthy lifestyle. Knowing when anxiety becomes overwhelming is essential for keeping a high quality and peaceful life. If you feel stressed every day or all day, you are feeling anxiety. If you're worrying too much, and it's interfering with your career, relationships, or other aspects of life, you need take it as an alarm and do something about it before it becomes unbearable. If your fear, worry, or anxiety is disturbing you and difficult to manage, talk to someone, see a therapist, pray, exercise, listen to praise music, meditate on the word of God, do something creative, do not sit in that that you feel.

Gratitude journaling is a simple approach to acknowledge what we are grateful for in our lives on a daily basis. The simple act of focusing on what you're grateful for and then listing it out may be an eye-opening exercise in recognizing the bounty that surrounds us every day. Taking the time to pause and reflect on what you're actually grateful for right now can have a significant impact on how you feel about your life. Personally, when I focus on gratitude, I am able to see what is instead of what is not. When I focus on the thing causing me anxiety, my mind creates things that are not there, I create things that could happen or may result, and it is never good. I concentrate on the source of the anxiety; it's like mediating on the source of the anxiety instead on the word of God or on something good and positive. Gratitude, though, helps me switch my thoughts from those frustrating things to things for which I am grateful. If I think too much about the frustrating things it seems they get more power and my mind spirals thinking of more and more negative and frustrating things. Focusing on gratitude does the same thing but in a good or positive direction. My mind spirals and thinks of more and more good things.

When can you make time to write in your gratitude journal? For me I write better in the morning after prayer and meditation to help get my day off to a good start and my day is focused so that I bring more and more good thoughts into my day. Be specific so your general thoughts won't get repetitive. Being specific is important. It helps you identify the small things as well as the big things and everything thing you are grateful for in between.

It is important that I show gratitude for the good things. So, I make sure God hears my words of gratitude and sees that I am grateful in my actions. Like love, gratitude is a noun, a feeling or idea, in this respect thoughts are certainly important. But it should transform into action, I am from the show me school, and I think God is too, since I am created in his likeness. Stop telling me, and show me. So, I feel like He wants me to tell Him that I am grateful AND to show him. So,I thank Him daily, sometimes briefly all day, throughout the day as thoughts and situations occur. Prayer, meditation, praising God, helping others, being kind to myself, spending time in nature, using my talents and resources to help others, are ways I show my gratitude to God.

Did you know that our brains actually transform when we show gratitude? Parts of the prefrontal cortex activates and "feel good" chemicals, such as dopamine and serotonin, are released. Through this process, we become more receptive to the positive aspects of life and more fulfilled by our relationships with others. Gratitude is so important. A continuous focus on gratitude also helps us gravitate toward warm and receptive emotions in the long term.

Gratitude Reflections

Focus on the happy childhood memories because they feed well-being in adulthood in a healthy way. Whereas, focusing on the trauma helps feed sadness, anxiety, and depression. And it sometimes causes you to be unproductive.

1. What is a happy memory from your childhood?
2. As you reflect on this happy memory, allow yourself to travel back in time.
3. Describe the sights, sounds, and sensations that surrounded you.
4. What made that moment so special?
5. How did it make you feel?
6. What life lessons or lasting joy did the memory give you?

7. How do you show you trust God?
8. What can you do to stay strong, steadfast, and consistent?
9. Who in your immediate circle should you talk to more or spend more time with?

It is okay to think about lessons learned from the negative stuff, but give the good memories more attention. Early experiences that distill sincere affection and attention are like seeds that nurture psychological health. Likewise, few experiences are more exciting than a childhood full of joy, discovery, and special experiences that we always like to remember.

Of course, therapy is important, but an attitude of gratitude coupled with I AM statements are great ways to heal your inner child trauma. These are tools used to reframe your negative self-talk and curb anxiety. With enough practice, they really do work to re-train the brain to adapt an overall encouraging mentality helping you to be more productive. What do you appreciate about yourself? Reflect on your gratitude for your best traits like body type, physical assets, personal qualities, achievements, or aspects of your character that you value, and everything about you. Your gratitude could range from your sense of humor, your resilience in tough times, you could be grateful for your willingness to help others, or to get things done. Your gratitude can range from your outer beauty, and yes, it is okay to thank God for making you physically beautiful. Be grateful for a recent accomplishment, a good choice you made, or even your abilities, no matter how small. Consider how these traits have positively impacted your life and why it's important to recognize and appreciate these aspects of yourself expressing gratitude. There is a gratitude journal worksheet to get you started in the useful tools section as the back of the book.

2 Chronicles 15:7 "Be ye strong therefore, and let not your hands be weak: for your work shall be rewarded."

Worry is usually about the future, overthinking what hasn't happened yet. While trauma is usually about the past, things that have happened and you can't change. When we are full of anxiety and feeling depressed we rarely focus on the present. If we do think about the future as a depressed person, we add doom and gloom to our future. I was a chronically depressed person for most of my life, including childhood. This was mostly because I was lonely as there were many children in our house but none of them were in my age range, I was the eldest, so I did not consider them good company. They had each other but I was usually the babysitter, the one in charge. I was very shy because I stuttered badly so I didn't have many friends outside of the home. The other reason I was depressed as a child is because my father left home when I was about seven or eight and I spend most of the remainder of childhood grieving his presence. Then stress that came with adulthood, then a difficult marriage, raising children, then a challenging business only accelerated my anxiety. Although changing my thoughts increased my coping skills. I didn't learn to reduce my anxiety by simply changing my thoughts alone; I needed to add self-reflection and self- awareness as a strategy to help learn to cope, find happiness, and joy. Anxiety has lessened for me as I learned to cope by using my body to calm my mind instead of relying on my mind to calm my body so I could do the work God put in my heart and do it with all my might. I find it interesting that in the midst of depression and anxiety, the Lord allowed me to find my purpose, but I could not do it well being depressed.

When I learned to self-reflect, I thought, "whatever the Lord put in your spirit to do, do it with your might! Don't let your mind or the mind of others weaken your hands to do the work you are put here to do! How does this keep you strong in God?" At some point in life, we all face situations that can test our resolve and leave us feeling discouraged. Whether it's a broken relationship, a challenging job, an unattainable goal, or an elusive dream, the temptation to give up can be overwhelming. Thankfully, God has given us a promise in **2 Chronicles 15:7** that can serve as an encouragement in times of difficulty, "But as for you, be strong and do not give up, for your work will be rewarded." Use this passage as a gratitude journal entry, and as you write this journal entry, explore the meaning of this verse by reading all of **2 Chronicles 15**, the whole chapter. This chapter can help you stay strong in your faith and persevere in your pursuits. Azariah, the son of Oded, received the Spirit of God and went to see Asa. He told him, "Hear me, Asa, and all Judah and Benjamin; The Lord is with you while you are with him; and if you seek him, he will be found of you; but if you forsake him, he will forsake you." Like the people during the previous reign of Abijah an unrighteous king and Asa a righteous king's time though, we have to rid our lives of all idols and false doctrines for good. We can't make this mistake, we can't keep going back and forth. Are we going to serve God or not? Unfortunately, we don't have control over "we" or "us" our control is only over "I, me, and my life."

Self-Reflection
- How do you show that you trust God?
- What can you do to stay steadfast and consistent in your efforts to make your calling and election sure?
- How can you remain grateful and use it as a tool for continuous growth?

Additionally, always express gratitude and appreciation to your family, friends, and co-workers. Learn to appreciate what you do well and learn to accept accolades from others for your good works. Oftentimes, we downplay complements, they make us uneasy because we don't appreciate ourselves. This is also part of self-reflection. When anyone in your circle does things that make you feel appreciated, you should let them know how their acts affected you. This allows them to gain a better understanding of you and increases their capacity to support you later on. This can also lead to greater levels of warmth and vulnerability in your relationships, ultimately strengthening them over time. A simple "thank you" or "I appreciate you" is often enough to make some feel your gratitude. As an educational leader, I learned that I could get my staff to buy into my mission for our students and our institution by complementing the on their work and making sure they know how I appreciate them. Appreciation is a game changer for families, institutions, churches, and business. It is a form of gratitude.

Trust God Over Your Emotions

Listen to God instead of your feelings. Your emotions may fluctuate, but God's truth never changes. It's important not to repress your feelings; feel them freely as God created you as an emotional being. However, it's equally important to test your feelings. Only those that bring you closer to God provide an authentic picture of your circumstances.

If your emotions lead you to do something that separates you from God, it reflects incorrect thinking that is out of touch with reality. Always choose to do what is right, no matter how you feel at the time. Determine where you are on life's path and ask God for what you require in that particular part of your path. Every person's journey through life includes destinations comparable to those described in the Bible as God leading the Israelites. Examine where are you in your journey right now. You could be in "Egypt," where you're bound, out of control, oppressed, or estranged from God's presence. You could be "encamped," where you're waiting. You could be in the middle of a storm waiting for it to pass. In either place, pray that God quiets your feelings so you can hear is directions and the path he thinks best for you, your gifts, skills, and talents.

You may feel like you can do this alone, like you don't need anyone. Don't trust your feelings because everyone needs community. Remember, he called for the cunning wailing women, there was more than one woman called to pray for the nation. Connect with other cunning wailing women in the best possible manner. Learn how to relate to others in the unique ways that God has designed you to do so. Keep in mind that you should live just to satisfy God, not other people. In this way, you learn to satisfy yourself too. So, don't be concerned about what others think of you if you're truly going where God leads you. Be open with others, but set limits to protect yourself from emotionally and spiritually dangerous people who do not value you as God does. Determine your preferred social setting. Whether you prefer to meet with people individually, in small groups, or in large groups, your primary relationship structure is leading, partnering, or serving others in God. In that community, pray God helps you identify the needs you feel compelled to help meet.

On some days and in some periods of time, God may appear silent, as you try to make decisions for your life, doors are not opening for you to move forward, or you need to rest or heal. Don't let those feelings lead you. Take a pause to pray and meditate on the word for clarity and direction. Alternately, you may be hanging on, or you feel compelled to take the next step. You may think that God appears to be speaking to and directing you, doors may open for you to move forward, or you may sense the need for change. Change is sometimes difficult or downright uncomfortable. Take a pause to pray and meditate on the word for clarity and direction. Likewise, you could feel like you are in a peaceful place, the "Promised Land," where God is fulfilling a desire or answering a prayer. You might feel like you're home, you may feel glad, looking forward to additional benefits, or enthusiastic about owning and defending what God has given you. Wherever you are right now, ask God for what you need and trust He will provide it. Take a pause to pray and meditate on the word for clarity and direction.

Healthy relationships are important. Nurturing relationships are essential for emotional well-being and general brain health. Take time to reflect on your role as daughter, your role as sister, your role as student, your role as aunt. Prioritize your relations and reflect on what you can do to improve those that are important to you. Remember that very often the smallest acts can have the great impact. The relationships we will study here is sisterhood. Your relationships with other praying sisters can be gratifying and satisfying. Finding people who care about you, pull you up, sharpens your iron, and make you feel fulfilled is incredibly special. However, finding this requires some level of self-awareness. Understanding your role in these connections is essential for cultivating meaningful, long-lasting friendships and praying partners. If you expect friends to be vulnerable with you, you must also be willing to be vulnerable with them. Examine what makes a good friend, how to assess your abilities, and some tips for enhancing friendships in sisterhood. Our prayer partners become friends sometimes for a brief time but often for a lifetime. Although we pray about our own traumas and the traumas of others, we are not bound by trauma, we are bounded by prayer, and service to others through our intercessory prayers.

Sisterhood friendships are never one sided. To evaluate your potential to be a good friend or a good prayer partner, it's important to first understand what genuine friendship means to you. You might be the friend who always works to make occasions enjoyable, ensuring everyone has a good time. Your key traits of empathy, organization, and respect are crucial in this. Whatever your role in the friendship, use self-reflection to examine your role, your boundaries, and your strengths, and your areas of growth. Friendship is most vital when intimate truths can be shared with confidentiality and when mistakes are made, discussion can happen and forgiveness flows often. Trust and honesty are crucial components of friendship. With self-reflection, understanding the kind of friend, you aspire to be can guide you in assessing the kind of friend you are, giving you a sense of purpose in your friendships.

Equally crucial to friendships is the type of friendship your friends want and understanding their role as well. It is critical for friends to establish a compatible match. You may notice that your friends see you as the person to turn to when they are down. In this scenario, it is critical to consider your feelings about the role. Does it satisfy you, or does it leave you wanting more? Is there anything you cannot tell friend? Can your friend sharpen your iron? All of these are crucial factors to consider. **Proverbs 27:17** "Iron sharpeneth iron; so a man sharpeneth the countenance of his friend." It is our duty as part of our role as ambassadors for Christ to sharpen one another, to keep each other encouraged, and to not uphold each other in wrong. This passage reminds me of two iron rods rubbing against one another. They can produce a spark between them because of the increased heat created by the friction. We should sharpen one another. There is a wealth of knowledge and guidance on leading a good life in the book of Proverbs. In addition to teaching us to live moral lives as individuals, it also teaches us to live as a community, working to support one another as we deepen our relationship with God.

Apply prayer when faced with determining how you can best contribute to the world while honoring God. Trust the Father to guide you in the greatest ways to relate to and serve others. Do whatever God wants you to do with your life? Each day, focus on accomplishing exactly what God wants you to do, at the right time, and with love. Take a pause, pray, and meditate on the word. Learn to let God lead you. Do not create unrealistic goals; reflect on your selections and don't be afraid to alter your goals when necessary. Make goals that are realistic for your lifestyle and simply do your best. Keep in mind that the process of finding who and what God created you to be and putting it into action will last your entire life. Each step you take brings you closer to realizing God's plan for your life instead of following your feelings alone. Sometimes thinking through thoughts that create feelings may or may not be based on truth. That is where God comes in. That is when you need to pray for confirmation. Pause, think about the word, and pray. Allow God to guide you.

Spend more time in the present instead of past or even future. **Matthew 6:34**, "Take therefore no thought for the morrow: for the morrow shall take thought for the things of itself. Sufficient unto the day is the evil thereof." The past no longer exists and there is nothing you can do to alter it. Go through the motions of accepting it, letting it go, forgiving yourself as well as those you need to forgive. Remember, you might be able to have a conversation with these people nor get an apology, but forgive anyway. Furthermore, the future does not exist yet and any thoughts we have about it is created, since it has not happened yet. Currently, the future is a story at this point. It is more relevant to spend your valuable time being concerned about the present. The present is where we can make effect changes which impacts your future. Consider how you typically handle disagreements and arguments with friends. Many of us struggle to share our relationship requirements with others because it makes us feel vulnerable; nevertheless, remember that your friends should also want meaningful relationships right now, with you. True friends and concerned family, the ones who truly care about you, will be concerned about your damaged feelings and strive to help them feel better. We don't want to accept criticism, even when it is constructive. It's also a good idea to consider how you usually handle feedback from others right now in the present.

When someone thinks you've hurt their feelings, resisting the desire to defend yourself is crucial. If you know to expect the feedback, instead of being offended by it, you can more likely set that temptation to feel offended aside accept that everyone's experiences and feelings are valid. Be willing to participate in a thoughtful restorative apology not long after the moment of conflict. Consider how you typically handle disagreements and arguments with current conflict. Many of us struggle to share our relationship requirements with others because it makes us feel vulnerable; nevertheless, remember that your friends should also want meaningful friendships with you. True friends, the ones who truly care about you, will be concerned about your damaged feelings and strive to help them feel better. It's also a good idea to consider how you usually handle feedback from friends. When someone thinks you've hurt their feelings, do not ignore their feelings. Be an active listener, their feelings determine their mood and their feelings matters. Their feelings are also valid, neither of you can allow them to overtake you causing darkness in your brain.

Whatever you can do to control the things that cause your feelings to be sad, lonely, angry, critical, or even jealous, do it, control it, change it. However, if you have no control, do not meditate on the negative thoughts and emotions. Don't be tempted to give the negative too much attention. It will spread through the amygdala part of your brain and both your body and your environment, including the people around you, will respond negatively. Drown the negative with positive thoughts. Understand that gratitude are the most powerful thoughts you can use to drown the negative out. Resisting the desire to defend yourself is crucial. If you know to expect constructive feedback, you will be more likely to set that temptation aside and participate in a thoughtful apology not long after the moment of conflict. Speak life into your feelings by practicing positive self-talk. Make this a habit by practicing it on a daily basis. Your thoughts are seeds, so plant good ones. You have the power to fix struggling relationships with important people in your life right now in the present. This practice will help you take an initial task as you learn to step into your power.

The initial step toward becoming a better person or companion is to own your flaws. Remember to exercise self-acceptance while doing so. We all have aspects of camaraderie and connection that are tough for us. That's part of being human. You can still seek for self-improvement. It is acceptable to believe both of these facts at the same time. Self-reflection is imperative to learning to cope.

You need to develop healthy friendships with your prayer partners in order to strengthen yourselves as praying women who pray for families, community, and then nation. Remember this is what God called for the Jeremiah 9 Women to do, pray for the nation. Imagine what God saw in those women, undergo your self-reflective process, and practice walking in that way so He also sees you. Self-reflection is a means of self-examination for continuous growth. **2 Corinthians 13:5** says, "Examine yourselves, whether ye be in the faith; prove your own selves. Know ye not your own selves, how that Jesus Christ is in you, except ye be reprobates?" Self-reflection can improve friendships by bonding you and your prayer partners to one another, develop empathy and understanding for others, while increasing authenticity and communication. As you initiate your self-examination as you continue to reflect, refer back to your list of characteristics of the 3 Prototypes of Godly Women. Let the 3 prototypes, Proverbs 31, Jeremiah 9, and Titus 2 women continue your self-reflection and guide you in the process. Self-reflection can be critical to helping you overcome trauma, including personal growth, self-awareness, decision-making, emotional intelligence, mental health, recovery, decision-making, and personal accountability.

We all have bad habits we want to break or need to break. Either way, planning, motivation, and goal-setting can help make breaking old behaviors possible even when it may seem impossible. "Let no man despise thy youth; but be thou an example of the believers, in word, in conversation, in charity, in spirit, in faith, in purity." **1 Timothy 4:12** tells us the importance of setting a godly example and accountability in breaking bad habits. Following Paul and Timothy's example, we can overcome negative habits through righteous leadership, mentorship, and discipleship. When you examine the disciples, we see they were learners and teachers. They knew when to follow The Master teacher and they went to lead sharing his teaching as they went from place to place and town to town as ambassadors of Christ sharing the good news of the gospel. In everything, set yourself up an example by doing what is good and what is right. In order to be a good example, we probably need to rid ourselves of bad habits we have developed over time. Some of our habits are sinful, some are just bad habits. **1 Corinthians 15:31**, "I protest by your rejoicing which I have in Christ Jesus our Lord, I die daily." Do a deep self-reflection so that at least those habits that are sinful can die and we can rid ourselves of them.

Self-Reflection

- What habits do you have that God would not approve of?
- What habits do you want to break?
- Which of your bad habits are tied to trauma or emotion?
- When it comes to my bad habits, where do I struggle with time, energy and excuses?
- What lessons do I need to learn?
- What steps do I take first, next, last?

Take it slow, make your list of habits you want to break, prioritize the list, then focus on one bad habit at a time. Add them to your goals and your prayer list. Figure out a reward system for yourself. Ask your prayer group to pray for that you break these habits. Talk to God about it. "His mercy endureth forever," and His grace is His gift to us. Even though scientists say it can take anywhere from 18 to 254 days, and 66 days on average, to change our behavior, we can become conquerors of our bad habits. We can do it quickly, or it may take a while, but we can do it because God, our strength, is always with us and there is nothing impossible with Him. Step into the power of God.

For Personal Growth

Reflecting on past experiences can help you understand your thoughts, emotions, and behaviors, which can help you identify your strengths and weaknesses. This awareness can help you develop new skills and improve existing ones. **Ecclesiastes 1:11** "There is no remembrance of former things; neither shall there be any remembrance of things that are to come with those that shall come after." After learning what it is you need to learn from mistakes and traumatic experiences, try to ease your thoughts of the bad experiences, do no meditate on the, cast them out, be an influencer of your own negative thoughts. Mark the good moments and the blessings, so you can remind yourself of God's love for you and how he has gotten you out of bad times. This will build you faith so you remember that he will get you out of this current situation too. Be grateful, remember it is a game changer.

As a Path to Self-Awareness

Self-reflection can help you improve your self-awareness, which can lead to self-improvement. It can also help you identify characteristics that aren't shared with others, which can help you understand your personal identity. We have to keep **Romans 12:3** in mind as we become more self-aware. "For I say, through the grace given unto me, to every man that is among you, not to think of himself more highly than he ought to think; but to think soberly, according as God hath dealt to every man the measure of faith."

For Better Decision-Making

Self-reflection can help you make better decisions for yourself by helping you evaluate your options and how they will impact you. As you are making decision, think of **2 John 1:8** Watch out that you do not lose what we have worked for, but that you may be rewarded fully.

For Emotional Intelligence

Self-reflection can help you understand and process your emotions without acting on them. **Proverbs 3:5-6** tell us to: "Trust the Lord with all your heart, and do not lean on your own understanding. In all your ways, acknowledge him, and he will make straight your paths." It's essential to recognize Christ's emotional intelligence and the role He has in our sense of well-being and confidence.

To Improve Mental Health

Self-reflection can improve your rest and mental health. For example, writing down your feelings in a journal can help you sleep if you're having trouble sleeping due to anxiety or worries. As you reflect on your situation and how you feel about it, do a commandment check. How do your actions and behavior recently align with God's commandments? The Bible does not speak directly to mental illness apart from **Deuteronomy 28:28** which reads, "The Lord will strike you with madness and blindness and confusion of heart." Here, God was warning the Israelites about rebelling and worshipping the Canaanite gods. Mental illness would be one of the results of rebellion. Reflect on the goal, to become a praying woman. You will be a better praying woman when you improve your mental health and rid yourself of depression and anxiety.

Self-Reflection Towards Recovery

Self-reflection can be an important part of whatever it is you are recovering from because it can help you identify your emotions, feelings, beliefs, and values, and stop to think about your stressors, motivations, and addiction. In many cases, at the foundation of addiction is fear, hurt, or anger. Human anger and negative emotion do not produce the righteousness that God desires. James 1:20. "For the wrath of man worketh not the righteousness of God."

Anger might temporarily improve our mood by giving us the impression that we have control over the people in our lives. However, this comes at a hefty cost, even if one is not spiritual. When we live out of rage, we lose our self-control, honesty, and other people's trust. Above all, it prevents us from praying and staying connected to our source, then God cannot draw close to us.

To Promote Better Decision-Making Skills

Self-reflection can help you make better decisions for yourself. Understanding yourself better can help you evaluate all your options and how they will impact you with more clarity. This can help you make sound decisions that you're more comfortable with. **James 1:5** "If any of you lack wisdom, let him ask of God, that giveth to all men liberally, and upbraideth not; and it shall be given him. Remember to keep praying because practice makes your prayers effectual and remaining in sincere prayer makes your praying fervent." **James 5:16**, "The effectual fervent prayer of a righteous man availeth much."

As a Means for Greater Accountability

Self-reflection can help you hold yourself accountable to yourself. It can help you evaluate your actions and recognize personal responsibility. It can also help you hold yourself accountable for the goals you're working toward. **Romans 14:12**, "So then every one of us shall give account of himself to God. **James 5:16**, "Confess your faults one to another, and pray one for another, that ye may be healed." Your praying partners should be willing to hear your confessions and pray through your faults as you work through them.

6

Praying Through Trauma

rauma, because of family dysfunctions during childhood, extend far into adulthood when the trauma is not addressed and it influences various aspects of life. Adults often face challenges in personal relationships, the workplace, and their emotional well-being are sometimes plagued by this childhood trauma. It is the trauma we've experienced that helps to dictate who we are today. Sin in the result of unhealed trauma and it could be the very thing that disallows us from earning salvation. This is a good reason why it is imperative that we learn to deal with our trauma and overcome it. A good therapist can help you learn to overcome negative character traits caused by past trauma. However, through self-reflection, establishing clear boundaries, practicing gratitude, finding a group of praying sisters who can provide you with community, and let's not forget seeking therapy, that we take on the life long process of healing from the trauma.

The continuation of trauma and passing it on to our children, is what allows the curses to continue. Break the generational cycle starting with you helping yourself heal and increase your discernment helping you to make better choices by taking it to the throne and paying. It takes 2 years to completely heal our nervous system from any trauma using all the tools in our tool box: with herbs, supplements, honest journaling, restorative discussions with family and friends, therapeutic readings, studying the word, prayer, confession, humming, praising God, and meditation causing our thoughts to shift, to ease, and calm the negativity inside us. Redirect your trauma narrative because it has a direct impact on how you interact with the community of which you are part of. These tools are helpful in nourishing your nervous system and making you better able to release trapped emotion and negative thinking causing us to sin. Learn to release trapped trauma and take negative thoughts captive. Try herbal, vitamin, and mineral supplements, and pray a pray of healing for your mind. Take care of your mental health before it becomes a serious problem.

- Do you have unhealed trauma?
- Are you stressed?
- Do you have feelings of anxiety?
- Are you trapped in a depressed or hysterical mindset?
- Are you trapped in sin, fear, doubt, or sadness?

Reflecting on Procrastination

Understanding the close relationship between procrastination and childhood trauma is a crucial step in overcoming its effects on self-sabotage and personal development. As we delve into strategies to combat procrastination, it's important to emphasize the value of self-compassion. Starting small and finding a balance between safety and progress are also key elements in this journey. Self-compassion and is not a sign of weakness, but a powerful tool in your arsenal. We have to learn to forgive ourselves, in some cases before we can forgive others, we need to forgive ourselves.

Many people view procrastination as a lack of willpower, laziness, or a bad habit that needs to be broken. However, procrastination might be far more difficult for people who have gone through traumatic experiences as children. Childhood trauma causes the brain to rewire itself into a survival mode that is hyper-vigilant and perpetual, which is the link between procrastination and trauma. One's capacity to initiate and finish projects may need to be improved by this fear of uncertainty, the need for control, and making mistakes. Then, procrastination turns into a defensive strategy that makes it challenging to overcome distress and accomplish tasks leading to one's goals.

By realizing the connection between procrastination and early trauma, we may release ourselves from its hold and design a more meaningful and worthwhile life. Procrastinators are often guilt-motivated people because they can't find the consistent motivation to execute tasks, so instead, their work is fueled with anxiety and guilt. When you realize your childhood trauma is the cause of your tendency to procrastinate, you need first to forgive your parents. Realize therapy is a good thing. Whether your parents caused you childhood trauma willingly or unwillingly, your first step is to ensure you forgive them. Keep these scriptures in mind when attempting to overcome procrastination because of trapped trauma.

Ephesians 5:15-17 in mind when you think about the tendency to procrastinate. Let the word of God be your balm. "See then that ye walk circumspectly, not as fools, but as wise, Redeeming the time, because the days are evil. Wherefore be ye not unwise, but understanding what the will of the Lord is."

Proverbs 13:4 "The soul of the sluggard desireth, and hath nothing: but the soul of the diligent shall be made fat."

Proverbs 12:24 "The hand of the diligent shall bear rule: but the slothful shall be under tribute."

Proverbs 20:4 "The sluggard will not plow by reason of the cold; therefore, shall he beg in harvest, and have nothing."

The fact that your parents may have argued in your earshot caused you childhood trauma. When you and your spouse argue fiercely in front of your children, it causes them trauma. This is how we pass generational trauma to our children and their children. It is a chain reaction that spirals. How many times has this happened in the last month? When it happens inadvertently, understand that your parents may have experienced childhood trauma as well, and they probably did the best they could to prevent you from experiencing childhood trauma. Because of your trauma, you might feel intolerant of their experience, but be compelled to make a conscious effort to push that out of your mind. It is with understanding that you will be able to move away from it and not repeat the trauma they experience. It is well known that childhood trauma has long-term effects, reorganizing the brain, lowering self-esteem, complicating relationships, and sometimes causing physical and medical issues. The demanding aspect of parenthood may accentuate scars that persist despite efforts to heal from trauma's traces. It is your responsibility to make your calling and election sure by having a forgiving heart first. As a servant of God, we must honor our parents, whether they were good, excellent, or outstanding. Remember, it is the only commandment with promise. **Exodus 20:12**, "Honour thy father and thy mother: that thy days may be long upon the land which the LORD thy God giveth thee." I imagine that not only will our days be long, but they could be productive and pleasant as well. If you carry deep scars, father wounds, or mother wounds, remember that you are not alone. In severe cases, the word of God is not enough because church leaders have not been trained to help us apply the word to acute cases. In these cases, therapy can be a powerful tool in your healing journey, ensuring that you heal thoroughly. And remember, the Word of God can also be a source of restoration and renewal when you learn how to use it as such. **Psalms 147:3**, "He healeth the broken in heart, and bindeth up their wounds." We need ministers who are also willing to take the steps to become licensed therapists. Life is complex, and trauma is traumatic, and some ministers do not have the money or willingness to help the church use the word to heal emotional trauma. We can't always do it alone. This is where a community of praying women can help.

Too many of us in the church are stuck in a state of procrastination and mental instability. It could be fear of failure. Perhaps we relive past wrongdoings or trespasses against us, and our hearts harbor hurt or resentment from the pain and suffering we endured. It sometimes feels like heavy luggage that we grip with aching hands. God will heal all of that unnecessary baggage. He gave the church the ability to free ourselves from the unclean spirits that overtake us due to childhood trauma. **Matthew 10:1**, "And when he had called unto him his twelve disciples, he gave them power against unclean spirits, to cast them out, and to heal all manner of sickness and all manner of disease."

When anxiety and the dread of failing overcome people's motivation and self-control, which can be undermined by fatigue or distant consequences, procrastination sets in. Understand that procrastination is not a form of laziness. Procrastination should not be mistaken for laziness, idleness, or sloth. The word "procrastinate" comes from the Latin "cras," which translates as "tomorrow." It refers to putting off duty because you think it will be easier or more enjoyable, even if it is usually less essential or vital. When someone's desire to avoid exertion precedes their desire to act morally, optimally, or as expected, they are lazy. When someone's desire to avoid exertion precedes their desire to act morally, optimally, or as expected, they are lazy. However, if their desire is to avoid failure, they more than likely procrastinate because of trapped trauma. There is probably something they fear.

Colossians 3:23. "And whatsoever ye do, do it heartily, as to the Lord, and not unto men." This scripture is a good reminder for a procrastinator. When one procrastinates, they plan ineffectively. Whereas a lazy person typically lacks motivation and self-control and has no desire or perceived effort.

Proverbs 13:4, "The soul of the sluggard desireth, and hath nothing: but the soul of the diligent shall be made fat."

THE CONNECTION BETWEEN PROCRASTINATION AND CHILDHOOD TRAUMA

The video investigates the close relationship between procrastination and childhood trauma, highlighting the effects it has on self-sabotage and personal development.

Self-Reflecting on Procrastination

There is something you can do if you are a procrastinator. Develop an anti-procrastination plan that includes: studying a passage in your bible daily, setting prayer alarms, building good habits, achieving goals, increasing your motivation starting with your thoughts, disciplining yourself, and improving the quality of your life by focusing on what you can control. If you haven't started journaling yet, start now. Write the following components in your journal to begin developing an anti-procrastination plan. Begin with recalling your blessings from your past and present. Your plan should include the key elements, with a special emphasis on setting and achieving goals. Be detailed and specific as you develop your plan, and track your progress. Remember, as a servant of The Most High, your anti-procrastination plan is not just about personal growth, but also about breaking generational curses. Keep these scriptures in mind as you embark on the journey of ridding your immediate family of generational curses.

Proverbs 10:4 "He becomes poor who deals with a slack hand, but the hand of the diligent makes rich."

Numbers 14:18, "The LORD is longsuffering, and of great mercy, forgiving iniquity and transgression, and by no means clearing the guilty, visiting the iniquity of the fathers upon the children unto the third and fourth generation."

Exodus 20:5, "Thou shalt not bow down thyself to them, nor serve them: for I the LORD thy God am a jealous God, visiting the iniquity of the fathers upon the children unto the third and fourth generation of them that hate me;"

Generational Curses

Because we serve a merciful and mighty God, you can be the generation that begins to combat generational curses with your righteousness and your work to heal. So can I for my family. Let's do this, one family at a time. Include the members of your family who are willing in your process, pray for one another, and agree to let this be the end of the generational curse in your family. Additionally, if you have inadvertently caused your children any childhood trauma, it's not enough to focus solely on your healing. You need to take responsibility for your actions, apologize, and consciously change your behavior. Be their model. Involve them in the process if they allow you to. This act of personal responsibility by self-reflection is a powerful tool for healing generations, one person as a time. If your children need therapy, arrange it for them. Then, help them start their anti-procrastination plan. The Word speaks about sin affecting families for up to four generations.

When we capture our thoughts and change them, our feelings and behaviors will change. According to the Word, our thoughts are under our control.

SCRIPTURE MOTIVATIONS:
- 2 Corinthians 10:5-6
- Romans 12:2
- John 14:1

John 14:1 "Let not your heart be troubled: ye believe in God, believe also in me." The words "Let not".....starts John 14:1.....meaning we have control. We have the power to bring our thoughts into captivity. It's a choice.

Releasing Trapped Trauma

When we release trapped trauma, we take negative thoughts captive. This is a physical and spiritual process. We can find the trapped emotions from even our childhood and release it. We can get to the root cause instead of simply managing it. Releasing the trauma is a better way of coping. When you are feeling anxiety or thinking negative thoughts. Try this exercise.

1. Take deep relaxing breaths. Decide which breathing technique you will use.

2. Meditate on a short biblical passage of your choice, for example, **John 14:1**, "Let not your heart be troubled: ye believe in God, believe also in me." This will relax the nervous system.

3. Singing, humming, and laughing throughout the day will stimulate the vagus nerve, the main nerve in your parasympathetic nervous system, which can help you feel relaxed. The vagus nerve is a good research project. Singing, humming and laughing also increase your intake of oxygen which can help with improving energy and mood.

4. Move your body. Exercise can be a great way to relieve stress, regulate the nervous system, and help release trauma. Take a walk, practice stretching exercises, or dance around your living room to your favorite song. Physical activity may help release tension and help your body feel more relaxed, positioning your body to release trauma.

My sister, Dr. Margaret Sunni, taught me an Emotional Freedom Technique called tapping. So, when I feel negative emotions try to take over my thoughts she taught me to stop and TAP myself when I feel stressed. With 2 fingers, tap common areas of your face and chest while repeating a positive phrase such as "I completely and deeply love and accept myself. " Tap the outer palm, top of the head, side of the eye, center of your forehead, your temples, below your nose, and below your bottom lip and collar bone. under the arm. Tapping in this way releases trapped emotions. Look up more about EFT. Emotional Freedom Technique. It is also an interesting research project as you learn to deal with your trauma. Don't be reluctant to have peaceful and restorative conversations with family and friends who are willing. Remember, there is no shame in seeing a therapist.

Heal Your Nervous System with Supplements

Break your cycles: your life trauma, bad experiences, and today's perspectives with fallacy so they won't affect your children and continue the generational curses to the 3rd and 4th generations. Do what you need to do to heal your physical body of dis-ease and your brain of trauma while you learn to step into your power. Consult your doctor or natural health practitioner about herbs and supplements you need. Medina Nance, Naturopathic Herbalist, gave me a basic list of herbs and vitamin supplements for stress, anxiety, and depression reducing the effects of trauma. These supplements work for me. Talk to your health and wellness person about how these or other vitamins and minerals could impact your brain and how you deal with stress and anxiety.

1. Ashwagandha
2. Liquid Flaxseed oil
3. Magnesium,
4. B-Complex
5. Vitamin E with Selenium

Your health care practitioner may have different supplements to refer you to, the ones I listed work for me. Take proper care of yourself. Invest in your emotional, mental, spiritual, social, and physical well-being on a regular basis so that you can serve God and others effectively.

Matthew 22:37-40 "Master, which is the great commandment in the law? Jesus said unto him, Thou shalt love the Lord thy God with all thy heart, and with all thy soul, and with all thy mind. This is the first and great commandment. And the second is like unto it, Thou shalt love thy neighbour as thyself. On these two commandments hang all the law and the prophets."

It is the responsibility of every man and woman of God to apply the Bible. It cannot become just another book in your home or an unusable compilation of ancient manuscripts. Some people read the book to understand history or to acquire information about prophecy. We might see that in the camps we attend. If we don't put the word to use then what is the point of reading it. **Philippians 4:6** says, "Those things, which ye have both learned, and received, and heard, and seen in me, do: and the God of peace shall be with you." God is with us when we apply the Bible to our daily lives. We do not want to be among the tares God said allow to remain among us, we want to grow past that, change our behavior by applying the word of God, so we can be among the wheat. That is the goal.

Adult Coloring is a Meditative Process

Multiple sources praise the merits of coloring, a favorite hobby among youngsters for years. Adult coloring books are growing popular for people to unwind and reduce tension. Coloring may help you connect with your inner artist, relax, and find peace; it also works for adults. It is a simple pastime that helps get a person out of their head like a long drive, knitting, or handicraft can. It promotes joy, tranquility, and self-awareness while benefiting the brain. It helps to calm the mind and prevents ideas from entering. It helps to calm the mind, so you can control your thoughts and unproductive ideas from entering. Coloring allows you to focus on the easy task at hand. This meditation exercise can divert your focus from yourself and the things causing you stress. It calms the brain. When you concentrate on this simple exercise, your brain relaxes. You are not bothered by your thoughts and opinions. The hardships of life fade from your consciousness, and your body and brain may find this pleasurable. Coloring can boost your brain's capacity and preparing it to apply the tools and techniques discussed in this book.

Coloring is enjoyable, soothing, and sedative due to the minimal stakes involved. Whether you color beyond the lines, the results are unpredictable and prescriptive. It may be as organized or as wild as you like; it is tough to mess up. Its low-stakes nature contributes to its relaxing effect, and there are no consequences if you color beyond the lines. Adult coloring may be like a relaxing vacation rather than a challenging test of our talents. You will find color sheets to get you started at the back of the book under the valuable tools section.

TAKE A MEDITATION BREAK

1. Begin by simply taking a moment to thank God for your being and for taking care of you. Comprehend what gratitude feels like, simply giving thanks.
2. Choose your biblical mantra. Pick one short verse or one phrase from a scripture, change it as you see fit.
3. Find a quiet, comfortable place. You can be sitting or lying down. Choose a comfortable position.
4. Try simply sitting with your legs and arms uncrossed, your arms resting on your legs and feet on the floor so that you feel grounded.
5. The goal is to feel relaxed, comfortable and focused.
6. Decide if you want your eyes open or closed.
7. You can begin with taking deep breaths in through your nose and gently out of your mouth.
8. Slow your breath and take breaths in and out of your nose when you start your mantra.
9. Inhale the name of God (Malachi 3:16).
10. Exhale the phrase you chose from a scripture.

11. Be aware of other thoughts and emotions.
12. Accept the thought or emotions without judgement of self or others.
13. Now let it go, push it out of your mind.
14. Inhale the phrase you chose from a scripture.
15. Exhale the phrase.
16. Continue inhaling and exhaling the scripture you chose pushing out unwanted thoughts as you relax until your allotted time is done repeating the scripture silently in your head.

Meditation anchors you because it helps you keep His word first and foremost in your mind as those tornadoes (problems) blow through your life. Instead of looking at the circumstances around us, we can focus on The WORD of God. Instead of meditating on what the world says, and giving the mess too much energy, we can spend our time meditating on what God says. As we meditate, The WORD will get on the inside of us, flow through our brain, and begin to change our thoughts, our health and our reality! **Psalm 1:1-2** "Blessed is the man that walketh not in the counsel of the ungodly, nor standeth in the way of sinners, nor sitteth in the seat of the scornful. But his delight is in the law of the LORD, and in His law he meditates day and night." So, instead of finding His pleasures in the words or the ways or the fellowship of the wicked, the person who is truly happy finds pleasure in meditating on the Word and the ways of God ("Law," Torah, = instruction: God's Words about God's ways.). When you find that scripture that resonates with you and anchors you, meditate on it. Sometimes, depending on your circumstances, that anchor may change. That is why we need to keep our heads in the Word as much as we can so you know what is in there and you can easily find your anchor.

Learn to use **praise** as a weapon. Praising God is very Powerful. Why is Praise a Weapon? Let me first give a definition of praise. Praise is giving the highest honor you can offer to God. It is singing or saying your thoughts of love and awe to Him. Praise is worship, yet it is a particular form of worship. Like bowing before a king and exalting his greatness, praise is exalting God's perfection, goodness, and character, the greatness of the things He has done. Praise is weapon of warfare and deliverance, and praising God is more than that. It brings big benefits to us. It carries with it such potency for helping us fight and win our battles. The subject of praise brings us back to the importance tool called gratitude. Add gratitude to your praise. What do you have to be thankful for? When faced with a setback, stress trigger, frustration, or continuous worry, there is a tendency to engage in unhelpful self-talk or recurrent negative thinking, which has been related to growing levels of anxiety. The positive news is that thankfulness can lessen such thinking.

That's why it is called a weapon of **warfare and deliverance**. And oddly enough, this weapon is probably most effective when we're down, struggling, and just barely able to open our mouths. Something about that effort while under duress especially moves God's heart. Some writings say when we praise God it frustrates the heck out of the devil. He gets furious because with the first feeble word of praise offered, we start to get back up on our feet. Well, It sounds good but I couldn't find a scripture that supports that. I did however find where Satan believes in God and trembles. **James 2:19**, "Thou believest that there is one God; thou doest well: the devils also believe, and tremble." And check this out, **Psalms 22:3** tells us, "But thou *art* holy, O *thou* that inhabitest the praises of Israel." Let's unpack the work inhabitest, what does it mean? The base word is inhabit and it means to live, stay, and to settle. To be present and to occupy. I don't know about you but when tornadoes come my way, I have to stop myself from making my troubles bigger than God, and If I can focus on him and not them, If I can manage to meditate on his word instead of thinking too hard on them causing me to to ungrateful and forgetful, If I can manage to praise him in my meditations and let it come out of my mouth I am strengthened and I feel better. The situation doesn't feel so hard and it doesn't hurt so deep, my heart is not so heavy. I imagine it is because when I praise God settles in my space and he comforts me and gives me peace in the storm.

The bible calls praise a sacrifice. **Hebrews 13:15**, "By him therefore let us offer the sacrifice of praise to God continually, that is, the fruit of *our* lips giving thanks to his name." When you think about it, praise IS a sacrifice because when you are feeling badly, if you are sad, sick, angry or even full of fear praise is the furthest thing from your mind. We tend to praise God if we are feeling good, but praise does make you feel good. It relieves stress and anxiety. It changes your mindsets. Coupled with understanding the word of God, it is a healing balm. **Psalms 47:7** "For God is the King of all the earth: sing ye praises with understanding." It calms your anger, gets rid of your fear, and helps you fight your battles.

Praise is a weapon and reminds of **2 Chronicles 20:15**, "And he said, Hearken ye, all Judah, and ye inhabitants of Jerusalem, and thou king Jehoshaphat, Thus saith the LORD unto you, Be not afraid nor dismayed by reason of this great multitude; for the battle is not yours, but God's." Praise will break the strongholds that bind us. Praise breaks the chains that bind us. Praise is like a sword and is also your defense and your strength. Praise gives you the strength to stand your ground when faced with the enemy and the storms we encounter. I'm thinking praise is called a sacrifice because when in turmoil, we do not naturally think to praise God. So, we don't give in to our pain, but we offer it up, put it in the back of our minds, push ourselves to praise God instead of focusing on the problem. As a sacrifice, praise becomes a meditation, we give The Most High our energy and our focus instead of the pain. Praise is the key to loose power from heaven, pushes the storms back, and unleashes the resources of weaponry so we don't need to fight for ourselves. This is how I feel when I offer the sacrifice of praise allowing me to literally give the battle to the ones it belongs to, my Father and His son; Elohim. I feel as though The Most High is opening up the windows of heaven and pours His spirit down on me and I feel better about my problems, or they dissipate.

REFLECTING ON PRAISE AS A SACRIFICE

- What are your thoughts about praise?
- What is the sacrifice of praise spoken about in **Hebrews 13:15**?
- How do you magnify the Lord in your life?
- Does it surprise me that God is mindful of me? Why or why not. Use a scripture to support your why.
- How do you express praise and gratitude consistently to God?

Tap Into Spirituality God's Way

Spirituality is biblical. Serve God with all of your heart and mind. Include your resources like time, energy, talents, and even your money and staying focused on God will naturally follow. **Deuteronomy 6:5** "And thou shalt love the LORD thy God with all thine heart, and with all thy soul, and with all thy might." **Matthew 22:37** further states, "Jesus said unto him, Thou shalt love the Lord thy God with all thy heart, and with all thy soul, and with all thy mind." If we want to love God, we have to love Him exclusively. No other gods can hold our attention. Our hearts must be focused solely on what pleases His heart. Our minds must be grounded solely on His word as the final authority. Our spirits can only be happy with what pleases Him. And in serving Him, we find our strength and joy. Understanding what love means from a biblical perspective is important in order to serve God with all your heart, soul, and mind. The term "love" has numerous connotations and can therefore be applied to a variety of situations. There is love between a mother and her child, between friends, between family, romantic love between a man and a woman, and so on. When we discuss the great love that Jesus mentioned, certain scripture texts render it as steadfast love. It is known as perfect love, covenant love, authentic love, and unconditional love.

A Different Goal for Journaling

Use your journaling from this book to journal your testimony and share it with others at the time appointed. When we learn to "man up" through our storms then we have a testimony to share and we have a story to tell. Journaling can be a powerful tool to help you become more in tune with your thoughts and feelings. After spending time with an important friend or experiencing feast times or other events, it can be beneficial to write about the experience. This process can help you observe any emotions that arise. For instance, if you write about a how you have grown after participating in a women's retreat, you may feel more upbeat and appreciative. On the other hand, you may notice that a friend's teasing comment has crossed the line into cruelty. This self-reflection can prompt you to discuss this with your friend as soon as possible, preventing the development of resentment and fostering a more proactive approach to relationships. Journal about how to used the experience to build your character and draw close to God.

When you are ready to tell your story, publish it. Sharing your testimony could be the goal because it reminds you that you can weather any new storm and God will help you through them just as He has our past storms. As you use the self-reflections in this book they may prompt you more questions. Write them down and use them if you decide to publish your story. When you share your story it helps others, your story will strengthen them so they know that they can push through that they can make it to the end of whatever they are going through and come out with flying colors and walk in God's sunshine.

Following King David's confession at the beginning of **Psalm 51**, he promised to teach others about the ways of God and to praise His Name in the assembly. When he says, "I will teach transgressors Your ways, and sinners shall be converted to You," he speaks of the gratitude he would feel should God answer his prayer. That gratitude would motivate him to bring the message of salvation to others. He understood all too well what it was like to be in bondage to sin and to live in shame and disgrace before God's righteousness. Once God David, his response becomes one of intercessory and charity—to bring others to understand the good news of God's mercy. By spreading the good news of forgiveness in Christ, we proclaim the goodness and righteousness of God. Sharing your story helps spread the good news about how God helped you through storms. It is a show of gratitude and is another way to worship God. Do you feel compelled to tell others of the mercy of Christ? Start a gratitude journal. Write it down to help organize your thoughts. Use it to think through your testimony and to write your story so that when you are ready you have all the particulars already written, there is a record of your growth, and the journal can be used to teach others of God's mercy.

So, to recap, the capacity to "man up" is having faith in the might of the Lord and being strong in Him. to comprehend that He has the ability to alter circumstances, and that we must persevere in prayer until something changes. God is both our support and our strength and our help. Let's "Man Up" through the storms.

7

Step Into Your Power

Help and Serve Others

Proverbs 19:17 tells us, "He that hath pity upon the poor lendeth unto the LORD; and that which he hath given will he pay him again." Imagine what it could be like if God owes you good for your good. The word says we reap what we sow. **Galatians 6:7,** "Be not deceived; God is not mocked: for whatsoever a man soweth, that shall he also reap." This passage often has a negative connotation because of how we use, it. Usually we use it when we are reminding someone that the bad they do will come back to them bad. But what about the good, won't good come back to us as well? Of course, it will, God knows the intentions of our hearts, and He will repay us.

While helping others, be the one in your circle who encourages the people around you, **Hebrews 3:13** says, "But exhort one another daily, while it is called To day; lest any of you be hardened through the deceitfulness of sin." Charity is love and kindness can be used as tools for healing and a excellent examples of love. Kindness is spreading sunshine into other people's lives regardless of the weather through acts and giving. Be kind to others, and to family first. This is a way to love your neighbor as you love yourself. Love begins at home and spreads abroad. The scripture stated, "But if anyone does not provide for his own, and especially for those of his household, he has denied the faith and is worse than an unbeliever" **1 Timothy 5:8**. God is love **1 John 4:7-8**. In loving us, God continually shows us His mercy and kindness.

Consider how frequently you commit acts of kindness and provide support when needed. In relationships, it is critical to be warm and nice to others. When someone shares wonderful news, it is important to respond with enthusiasm. When someone met an accomplishment or reaches a goal, we need to show genuine enthusiasm and congratulate them. If you know someone who has had a terrible week, it is very thoughtful to offer to take them out to dinner, babysit the children for an hour or two, or simply pray with them. Consider how often you think about doing these kinds of things for your loved ones, as it is a crucial aspect of being an outstanding servant of God.

"Man-up" Through the Storm

We've all gone through a few tornadoes in our lives where if we did not man up and understand that God is more powerful than the situations, systems, or people who cause the storms, the troubles and the challenges we faced that we would not have been able to stand, because the storms were raging. I call these times tornadoes. Sometimes we have to remind ourselves that we have to remain anchored in the Lord. Do you recall the song, "My Soul Has Been Anchored In the Lord by Douglas Miller. These are the times we need to "man-up". When times are hard, when times are rough, when things just don't seem go our way. How do we man up? Let me count the ways. These are the 7 ways for women to "man-up".

1. Read the word
2. Pray
3. Meditate
4. Praise
5. Serve God with all our hearts

6. Help others
7. Share your testimony; tell your story; start a journal

These are seven ways to "Man-up" Through the Storm when life get to "life-ing". Remember, before you pick up the phone, go to the throne. Increase your faith, pray and trust God.

Read the word so you stay grounded. And you remember what He promised. His word is like an ointment for the wounds the storms causes. Stop, drop and pray several times each day. It does not have to be for hours, pray long enough to pour your heart out to God and petition for His help. It could be as simple and as quick as, "O Most High God heal my mind, wash it, cleanse it of negative thinking and renew it. Help my sisters in pray to draw close to you." Knowledge of God gained through Scripture is not identical with grace, but Peter says it is a means of grace. If we want to be made peaceful and powerful through divine grace, Peter says, it happens "in the knowledge of God and of Jesus our Lord." That knowledge is found in one place: in the Word of God.

Scripture sanctifies. Jesus said, sanctify them in the truth; your word is truth. **John 17:17.** "We're all assigned in some measure to handle the word of God." Sanctification is the process of separating yourself from things that are unholy and wrong and becoming holy — that is, becoming more like Christ, who is perfectly holy. This is not optional. **Hebrews 12:14** says, "Strive . . . for the holiness without which no one will see the Lord."

Scripture gives joy. You received the word in much affliction, *with the joy* of the Holy Spirit. **1 Thessalonians 1:6,** "His delight is in the law of the Lord, and on his law he meditates day and night. **Psalm 1:2,** "But his delight *is* in the law of the LORD; and in his law doth he meditates day and night." Life without joy is unbearable. The servants life can be a life of many afflictions. But in them all, God both gives and sustains joy, and He does it by the drawing close to Him. **2 Timothy 2:15** "Study to shew thyself approved unto God, a workman that needeth not to be ashamed, rightly dividing the word of truth." We need to know what the word says and how to separate ourselves from that which is not good and the only way we know what thoughts and actions and behavior is approved by him is to read his word. Pray and find the scripture that grounds you. Mine other grounding scriptures are **Psalms 34:17** and the entire chapter of **Psalms 78.**

Prayer. What is prayer and why should we pray? Prayer is *communication* with God. We do this by praising Him, confessing our sin before Him, thanking Him and asking Him for our needs and desires. Prayer is *communion* with our Creator. When we pray, we engage in loving fellowship with the Maker of heaven and earth. He has graciously invited us into a close covenant relationship with Him through the person and work of Christ. Prayer is central to the life of a servant of God. We are commanded to pray "continually", **1 Thessalonians 5:17** as we seek God and grow in intimacy with Him, drawing closer to Him. It is simple as in **1 Thessalonians 5:17**, "Pray without ceasing." There are many different things that compete for our time and attention. Our time is packed with people and duties, wants and aspirations, and responsibilities, all of which require energy. Despite it all, we need to commit to giving our attention to prayer several times a day.

Find scriptures that anchor you. Locate the promises God made to His people in His word and remind Him of those promises in your prayers. I tend to worry about my adult children a lot. If I am looking at their lives too closely and things look glim from my view, I have to remind myself of the promise God made to me.   These scriptures anchor me during those times. **Psalms 34:17**, "*The righteous* cry, and the LORD heareth, and delivereth them out of all their troubles." **Psalms 34:1** "Many *are* the afflictions of the righteous: but the LORD delivereth him out of them all." **Psalm 78:41-42** "Yea, they turned back and tempted God, And limited the Holy One of Israel. They remembered not his hand, Nor the day when he delivered them from the enemy." Anchor yourself in the Word of God. Through study, prayer, meditation, gratitude, and praise.

Prayer is a powerful weapon for spiritual warfare and gratitude is a fuel that empowers your prayer. You can unleash this power in your life by drawing close to God when you apply His word to your daily walk. Jesus prepared his disciples to function without him by teaching them, answering their queries, showing every type of appropriate ministry possible. He gave us access to his instruction, but it is not enough. We also need God's power. There are occasions in life when we rely on our own strength. When we do this, we walk outside of God's incredible power for us. We try to manipulate circumstances around us with our own ideas and our own power. This may not be intentional, but we are still acting out of self-reliance. Self-reliance fosters doubt and dread. When we rely on ourselves, we are telling God that we do not need Him or His strength. We need to learn to step into your God's power and teach others to do so also. God's strength comes to us when we surrender, trust, study, pray, and have faith in Him beyond everything and anyone else. Whether you realize it or not, God has a unique purpose for your life that He wants you to discover and pursue. He wants you to include Him, to consult Him as you pursue this purpose. He wants you to experience Him as your power.

Fasting, Your Supernatural Power

Matthew 17:21, "Howbeit this kind goeth not out but by prayer and fasting." Many of the biblical characters in the old and new Testaments fasted and had extraordinary experiences with God. While Paul's fast resulted in a deep divine calling, Daniel fasted until he had a breakthrough. Peter's fast led to a revelation and a vision, while Esther's fast brought her protection, gave favor for her entire nation. Fasting in used as a tool to resolve difficult circumstances. Cornelius' fast brought revival to his household while Jesus himself highlighted the effectiveness of fasting and prayer. Jesus said, "When you fast," in Matthew's gospel, suggesting that believers are expected to fast. Outside of the appointed fast, on the Day of Atonement, we are free to choose what we eliminate from our day or our meals, whether it be certain meals, gadgets, or fasting from social media. The advantages of fasting become clear after we really experience them for ourselves. From my experience and by evidence from the word of God, fasting without food or water are ways to rid our spirits and our lives of the most difficult things that plague our lives. **Matthew 17:21**, "Howbeit this kind goeth not out but by prayer and fasting." As Jesus, Peter, James, and John descend from the mountain, they come across a man who has a demon-possessed son. Despite their best efforts, the disciples failed to drive the demon out. Following their 'lack of trust,' Jesus corrects them and heals the youngster. Later, he informs his followers that only unwavering faith, intense prayer, and committed fasting can accomplish such a strong miracle, encouraging them to deepen their spiritual practices.

Fasting is also a biblical way to truly humble yourself in the sight of God. King David said in **Psalm 35:13**, "I humbled myself with fasting." Seeking God's face sincerely is what fasting is. It involves giving all of our might and will to God alone, who provides. Fasting was a common and necessary component of religious life in biblical times. In order to seek God's favor and direction, people frequently fasted in addition to praying and confessing their sins. According to **Leviticus 23: 26-32** afflicting the soul is eliminating food and water for a time. **Esther 4:16** states, "Go, gather together all the Jews that are present in Shushan, and fast ye for me, and neither eat nor drink three days, night or day: I also and my maidens will fast likewise; and so will I go in unto the king, which is not according to the law: and if I perish, I perish." It is important to not make an announcement when you fast, **Matthew 6:16-18**. If you are not fasting with your prayer partners for a particular reason, keep your fasting to yourself. Let it be between you and God, it is not a show. Moses fasted without food or water for 40 days in **Exodus 34:21** and the Master also fasted that long in **Matthew 4:2**. Fasting can happen for a day or for as long as you commit to.

By fasting, we can put God first or return Him to His proper place of being first if we've strayed from him. There are excellent results when we put God first. By bringing our flesh to the altar, fasting forces us to control our cravings and submit to God's will. Fasting is a discipline. It reminds us of the importance of not letting our flesh rule our lives, inspiring us to prioritize our relationship with God. The most consequential benefit of fasting is its ability to awaken the spirit of God within us and tap into His power. Fasting helps us overcome the distractions of daily life that hinder our encounters with God, allowing us to go deeper into the supernatural realm. One effective way to strengthen our relationship with God is to fast. It cultivates a heart of worship, enabling us to thank Him and show our appreciation. We make room for a closer, more satisfying relationship with Him when we put aside our hunger, thirst, and material wants to concentrate on His goodness and petition Him for our needs. Our relationship with The True and Living God is enhanced as our praise grows more sincere and real. Are you prepared to step into God's extraordinary power through the supernatural power of fasting, prayer and praise? Get your copy of the book, The Supernatural Power of Fasting and Prayer from Preacherhead Ministries using this QR code.

Self-reflection or Self-worship:

As we watch the foundation of the country be unraveled and the stage being set for its fall, it's a good time to self-reflect and be honest about making changes so we can make our calling and election sure. **Psalms 51:2** "Wash me thoroughly from mine iniquity and cleanse me from my sin." **1 John 1:7 & 9**, "But if we walk in the light, as he is in the light, we have fellowship with one another, and the blood of Jesus, his Son, purifies us from all sin. If we confess our sins, he is faithful and just and will forgive us our sins and purify us from all unrighteousness." Prayer for cleansing. Dear God, free me from the darkness that covers my spirit. Remove the bad energy that harms my being. Illuminate the path of my life towards light, love and inner peace. "Have mercy on me O Lord, according to your steadfast love. I know my sin… it is ever before me. Wash me, blot out my transgressions, cleanse me and create in me a clean heart." Pray the entire **Psalm 51** over yourself daily.

What is self-reflection?
I look at self-reflection as self-love as me digging out the things in me not like Christ, so "I die daily," and change me so I can experience God's love in this life and in the life to come that he is preparing for his servants. As I die daily, may others experience God in me when they experience me as I make attempts to grow in the fruit of the spirit. "Wash me thoroughly from mine iniquity and cleanse me from my sin. For I acknowledge my transgressions: and my sin is ever before me."

If I am self- reflective, I don't find it difficult to understand or acknowledge the feelings and perspectives of others.

As I continue to self-reflect, I think of scriptures like **Psalm 24:1-10** for example.
It is a good scripture to use as the foundation for self-reflection and meditation.
"He that hath clean hands, and a pure heart, who hath not lifted up his soul unto vanity, nor sworn deceitfully."

Here's a breakdown of the verse:

The idea of clean hands emphasizes the importance of moral and spiritual integrity as a prerequisite for approaching God.

 Lifting up your soul unto vanity refers to avoiding pride and self-importance and not seeking glory or validation from worldly things. Swearing deceitfully condemns dishonesty and the violation of oaths, emphasizing the importance of truthfulness and integrity.

 As you reflect on and meditate on **Psalm 24:1-10**, turn verse 4 into a few questions.

 What situations have occurred in the past that I need to repent for because my hands or heart was not clean? Are my hands clean today? What choices do I need to make in a situation that occurred today where I can choose to prove to The Most High that my hands are clean?

What are the actions of a pure heart? Are my thoughts clean? How do I know? What's my evidence?

Am I lifting my soul unto vanity? Do I need to rebuke the devil, so he flees? Am I swearing deceitfully in a particular situation I face today? Have I sworn deceitfully today and have I repented for it?

Questions for self-reflection:

What ideas, thoughts, and attitudes are in you that need to die? What is your choice: self-reflection or self-worship? How does God know your choice? What is the evidence? What good or bad did others see in me last month? Last week? Yesterday? What will ensure others see good in me today? Tomorrow? Next week?

What other scriptures can you use for self-reflection and what questions can you ask yourself that will prompt change.

What is self-worship?

It's an inflated sense of self-importance
It is an excessive admiration of or devotion to oneself. In self-worship one often puts oneself even over God as seen in arrogance, conceit, and stubbornness.

1 Samuel 15:23-26 tells us, "For rebellion is as the sin of witchcraft, And stubbornness is as iniquity and idolatry. Because thou hast rejected the word of the LORD, He hath also rejected thee from being king."

Further, self-worship is when one focuses on personal needs and individual desires above all else and all others. **One who worships self is constantly seeking attention, validation, and admiration from others. Enough is never enough and it's irritating and exhausting for others when it's constantly expected.**

Self-worship is if I decide to make no adjustments, and instead, I take on an attitude of "be me", "this just how I am", while everyone around me must adjust to me "being me" while the people who love and care for me are forced to walk on eggshells because of me. And I treat others as if they are beneath me lacking both compassion and empathy because "I am better than they are."
Self-worship is different from self-love and self-care, which are important for mental and emotional well-being. Healthy self-love involves recognizing one's worth and value while still being empathetic, compassionate, considerate, and respectful to others.

When I worship myself, I make no attempt to change for the betterment, and I can't grow in The Fruits of the Spirit. I make no attempt to adjust, and I have no intentions of growing in the fruits, building my character, or transforming into a better person. Instead, I take the attitude, "This is just how I am." Don't be stuck in your bad attitude and bad behavior. Lift yourself out of that pit of self-destruction quick, fast, and in a hurry.

I think it is important that as we as women continue to undergo the process of self-reflection, we take a close look at the new thing God said He created in earth from Jeremiah 31:22 "How long wilt thou go about, O thou backsliding daughter? for the LORD hath created a new thing in the earth, A woman shall compass a man." The question in this passage scrutinizes the integrity of females who claim to be women of God. When examining the question, words that come to mind are wavering, faithless, unfaithful, hesitate, renegade, wandering, proud, haughty, and pretentious. As a self-reflective exercise, take out your journal and define these words, then describe how they fit into the question.

I've heard people misconstrue the word compass, mistaking its meaning for the definition of surpass. To establish meaning for compass, look at a time when God gave the city of Jericho to Joshua and the men of war. The passage Joshua 6:3-4 says, "And ye shall compass the city, all ye men of war, and go round about the city once. Thus shalt thou do six days. And seven priests shall bear before the ark seven trumpets of rams' horns; and the seventh day ye shall compass the city seven times, and the priests shall blow with the trumpets." Using context clues in the two verses, Joshua and the men of war were instructed to walk silently around the city's secured gates for six days, and on the seventh day, the instructions changed. As they were to go around the shut-up city they were instructed to blow the trumpets. Imagine that as they circled the city for those six days, nothing and nobody could get in or out of the city.

Now relate that process to a woman and her husband. We can deduce that women are to surround their husbands silently most of the time; then take time to shout praises to Elohim for the blessings they have. This will prevent the enemy and his legions from breaking through that threefold chain, God, husband, and wife, making sure "he," the husband, is protected. It is through prayer and praise that we protect our husbands from the wiles of the devil. Ecclesiastes 4:9-12 Two are better than one because they have a good reward for their labor. For if they fall, the one will lift up his fellow: but woe to him that is alone when he falleth; for he hath not another to help him up. Again, if two lie together, then they have heat; but how can one be warm alone?" Like Ephesians 5:21, putting others' needs above their own, "Submitting yourselves one to another in the fear of God."

When a woman is married to a man of God who loves her as Christ loved the church and she puts his needs above her own while she is praying for her husband instead of whining, crying to others, complaining, and even running, because of her prayers, she leaves no place for the enemy to enter her marriage or her home. On another note, when I think of the fact that nothing can get into or out of a circle, it puts me in the mindset that nothing should be able to come in between your marriage. Moreover, when a woman is led by a merciful, kind, compassionate, and caring head who provides for her and is the protection for the difficulties of challenging people and circumstances, she is humbled. So, she naturally and automatically submits to his leadership because she loves how he treats her. In circumstances such as this, she even enjoys the submission. Step into your power sis. Matthew 19:6, "Wherefore they are no more twain, but one flesh. What therefore God hath joined together, let not man put asunder."

Amen.

8

Useful Tools

Remembering, Comprehending & Applying

1. What are the virtues of a Proverbs 31 woman as described in the passage?

2. Write a description of what a Proverbs 31 woman might look like in today's world.

3. What are the attributes of a Titus 2 woman as described in the passage?

4. Write a description of what a Titus 2 woman might look like in today's world.

5. What are the characteristics of a Jeremiah 9 woman as described in the passage?

6. Write a detailed description of what a Jeremiah woman might look like in today's world.

7. How can the characteristics of each woman of God be summed up in a few sentences?

8. As you begin a personal purge, what do you want to learn from each of these prototypes?

9. How did these women grow in the fruits of the spirit?

10. How do we assume each prototype wears the garment of salvation, the robe of righteousness, and other parts of the armour willingly and even joyfully?

Analyzing, Evaluating & Synthesizing

1. What can you infer from the directive that God gave the Jeremiah 9 woman to teach her daughters?

2. What kind of love does each prototype demonstrate?

3. We can also do a deeper dive into certain specific words like the meaning of "submit" or "love".

4. Compare and contrast the 3 female Biblical prototypes.

5. What consistent pattern of behavior does God see in your daily walk that could cause God to call you when he calls for women to pray?

6. How does each prototype present us with a list that challenges our actions, our integrity, and our daily walk?

7. Which prototype do you identify with or aspire to be? Why?

8. What purging have you done so far?

9. What further purging do you need to do?

10. What will be your process for growth to reach the depths of the prototype you selected?

Three Biblical Prototypes for Women

LIST 5-7 CHARACTERISTICS OF EACH PROTOTYPE.

Characteristics of a Proverbs 31 Woman

_____
_____
_____
_____
_____
_____
_____
_____
_____

Characteristics of a Jeremiah 9 Woman

_____
_____
_____
_____
_____
_____
_____
_____

Characteristics of a Titus 2 Woman

_____
_____
_____
_____
_____
_____
_____

Three Biblical Prototypes for Women

USE THE GRAPHIC ORGANIZER TO STUDY THE LIST OF CHARACTERISTICS
TO DETERMINE WHICH ONES OVERLAP

Proverbs 31 Woman

Jeremiah 9 Woman

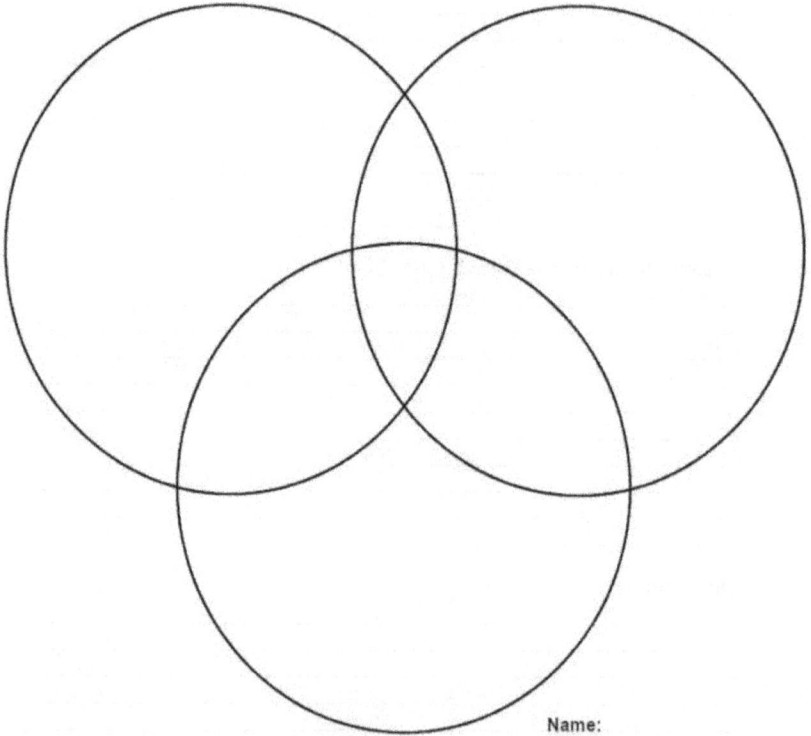

Name:

Titus 2 Woman

Three Biblical Prototypes for Women

1. After having finished the graphic organizer, write the characteristics which overlap.

2. Self-Reflection: Analyze both lists as they pertain to you. Which characteristics from your lists have you already developed?

3. Which characteristics do you need to work on?

4. Then prioritize that list on which you need to work. Group them according to similarities and differences.

Similarities	Differences

5. Can you work on any two or three one at a time?

6. Which do you need to work on alone?

7. Which will you start first? Why? What are the steps you need to take?

8. Do you have forgiveness to do? What steps can we take to forgive whomever and let go? Which characteristics did you identify in the 3 prototypes will you develop automatically when you forgive?

9. Your final list should focus on things you can do to build your character as a woman of God and a value to your sisterhood.

Biblical Prototypes

Proverbs 31 Woman	Titus 2 Woman	Jeremiah 9 Woman
Household	Next Generation	Nation

Useful Scriptures

Scriptures which Model Righteousness
Isaiah 61:10 "I will greatly rejoice in the LORD, my soul shall be joyful in my God; for he hath clothed me with the garments of salvation, he hath covered me with the robe of righteousness, as a bridegroom decketh *himself* with ornaments, and as a bride adorneth *herself* with her jewels."
Job 29:14 ."I put on righteousness, and it clothed me: my judgment *was* as a robe and a diadem."
Revelation 19:8 "And to her was granted that she should be arrayed in fine linen, clean and white: for the fine linen is the righteousness of saints."
Isaiah 59:17 "For he put on righteousness as a breastplate, and an helmet of salvation upon his head; and he put on the garments of vengeance *for* clothing, and was clad with zeal as a cloke."
Isaiah 11:5 "And righteousness shall be the girdle of his loins, and faithfulness the girdle of his reins."
Isaiah 64:6 "But we are all as an unclean *thing*, and all our righteousnesses *are* as filthy rags; and we all do fade as a leaf; and our iniquities, like the wind, have taken us away."

Important Scriptures About Friendship & Healthy Relationships
Proverbs 27: 17 Iron sharpeneth iron; so a man sharpeneth the countenance of his friend. Proverbs 18:24 A man that hath friends must shew himself friendly: and there is a friend that sticketh closer than a brother. Proverbs 16:24 Pleasant words are as an honeycomb, sweet to the soul, and health to the bones. Proverbs 17:9 He that covereth a transgression seeketh love; but he that repeateth a matter separateth very friends. Proverbs 12:26 The righteous is more excellent than his neighbour: but the way of the wicked seduceth them. Proverbs 22:24-25 24 Make no friendship with an angry man; and with a furious man thou shalt not go: 25 Lest thou learn his ways, and get a snare to thy soul. Proverbs 13:20 20 He that walketh with wise men shall be wise: but a companion of fools shall be destroyed. Ecclesiastics 4:9-13 9 Two are better than one; because they have a good reward for their labour. 10 For if they fall, the one will lift up his fellow: but woe to him that is alone when he falleth; for he hath not another to help him up. 11 Again, if two lie together, then they have heat: but how can one be warm alone? 12 And if one prevail against him, two shall withstand him; and a threefold cord is not quickly broken.

¹³ Better is a poor and a wise child than an old and foolish king, who will no more be admonished.

Job 42:10 ¹⁰ And the Lord turned the captivity of Job, when he prayed for his friends: also the Lord gave Job twice as much as he had before

Job 6:14 ¹⁴ To him that is afflicted pity should be shewed from his friend; but he forsaketh the fear of the Almighty.

James 4:11 ¹¹ Speak not evil one of another, brethren. He that speaketh evil of his brother, and judgeth his brother, speaketh evil of the law, and judgeth the law: but if thou judge the law, thou art not a doer of the law, but a judge.

Ephesians 4:32 ³² And be ye kind one to another, tenderhearted, forgiving one another, even as God for Christ's sake hath forgiven you.

1 Thessalonians 5:11 (The whole chapter of 1 Thessalonians 5 is a great read).

Wherefore comfort yourselves together, and edify one another, even as also ye do.

Ruth 1:16 And Ruth said, Intreat me not to leave thee, or to return from following after thee: for whither thou goest, I will go; and where thou lodgest, I will lodge: thy people shall be my people, and thy God my God:

Matthew 18:20 For where two or three are gathered together in my name, there am I in the midst of them.

James 4:8-10 8"Draw nigh to God, and he will draw nigh to you. Cleanse your hands, ye sinners; and purify your hearts, ye double minded. ⁹ Be afflicted, and mourn, and weep: let your laughter be turned to mourning, and your joy to heaviness. ¹⁰ Humble yourselves in the sight of the Lord, and he shall lift you up.

Insightful Prayers from Women in the Bible

Hagar's prayer for water reveals to us that God will provide our needs. (Genesis 16:6-14)
Miriam's prayer of praise reminds us that every triumph is the Lord's. (Exodus 15:19-21)
Deborah's prayer of God's glory demonstrates how God is at work in the great and small. (Judges 5:1-9, Judges 5:31)
Hannah's prayer for a child invites you to bring your heart's desires to God. (1 Samuel 1:10-16)
Esther's prayer gives us an example of how to ask others to pray for us. (Esther 4:15-16)
Mary's prayer of blessing shows how focusing on God's character offers our hearts joy. (Luke 1:46-55)

Important Prayers to Examine in the Old Testament

Abraham Genesis 20:17
Isaac Genesis 25:21
Moses (Exodus 9:30; Numbers 11:2, 21:7; Deuteronomy 9:20, 26; Psalm 90);
Manoah (Judges. 13:8),
Hannah (1 Samuel 1:11, 2:1-10); Samuel (1 Samuel 7:5, 8:6, 8:21);
David (2 Samuel 7:18-21; 1 Chronicles 17:16-27; Psalm 4, 5, 6, 17; Psalm 35:13; Psalm 39; Psalm 54; Psalm 55; Psalm 86; Psalm 109:4),
Solomon (1 Kings. 8:22-53; 2 Chronicles 7:1);
An unnamed "man of God" (1Kings 13:6);
Elisha (2 Kings 4:33, 6:17-20);

Hezekiah (2 Kings 19:14-19; 2 Kings 20:2-3;
Isaiah. 37:14-20, 38:2-3; 2 Chronicles. 30:18-20; 2 Chronicles. 32:20, 24);
Jabez 1 Chronicles. 4:10
"All peoples" who "join themselves to the Lord" (Isaiah 56:7);
God's people (Jeremiah. 29:7, 12); Jeremiah 32:16-25);
Cunning Women of Prayer (Jeremiah 9:17-20);
Jonah 2:1-10, 4:1-3);
Habakkuk 3;
Priests and Levites (2 Chronicles. 30:27);
Isaiah (2 Chronicles 32:20);
Manasseh (2 Chronicles 33:12-13);
Ezra 9:6-15;
Nehemiah 1:5-11, 2:4;
People of Israel Neh. 4:9; Job 16:17, 42:10;
Daniel 6:10, 9:4-19

Prayers in the New Testament

The Lord's Prayer – Matthew 6:9-13
Jesus' High Priestly Prayer – John 17
Prayer for Boldness of Witness – Acts 4:23-31
One of 3 Prayers in Ephesians – Ephesians 1:15-18
Second of 3 prayers in Ephesians – Ephesians 3:14-21
Third of 3 prayers in Ephesians – Ephesians 6:18-20
Prayer for the church of Philippi – Philippians 1:3-11
Paul's Prayer to Church of Colossae – Colossians 1:9-12
Prayer for All Men – 1 Timothy 2:1-8
Prayer for Gospel to Spread Quickly – 2 Thessalonians 3:1-5

The Power of Prayer

Mark 11:24 - Therefore I say unto you, What things soever ye desire, when ye pray, believe that ye receive them, and ye shall have them.

Philippians 4:6-7 - Be careful for nothing; but in every thing by prayer and supplication with thanksgiving let your requests be made known unto God.

James 5:16 - Confess your faults one to another, and pray one for another, that ye may be healed. The effectual fervent prayer of a righteous man availeth much.

John 15:7 - If ye abide in me, and my words abide in you, ye shall ask what ye will, and it shall be done unto you.

1 John 3:22 - And whatsoever we ask, we receive of him, because we keep his commandments, and do those things that are pleasing in his sight.

1 John 5:14-15 - And this is the confidence that we have in him, that, if we ask any thing according to his will, he heareth us:

Jeremiah 29:11-15 - For I know the thoughts that I think toward you, saith the LORD, thoughts of peace, and not of evil, to give you an expected end.

John 14:13-14 - And whatsoever ye shall ask in my name, that will I do, that the Father may be glorified in the Son.

1 John 5:14 - And this is the confidence that we have in him, that, if we ask any thing according to his will, he heareth us:

Ephesians 6:18 - Praying always with all prayer and supplication in the Spirit, and watching thereunto with all perseverance and supplication for all saints;

1 Timothy 2:5 - For there is one God, and one mediator between God and men, the man Christ Jesus;

Matthew 21:21-22 - Jesus answered and said unto them, Verily I say unto you, If ye have faith, and doubt not, ye shall not only do this which is done to the fig tree, but also if ye shall say unto this mountain, Be thou removed, and be thou cast into the sea; it shall be done.

Matthew 6:9-13 - After this manner therefore pray ye: Our Father which art in heaven, Hallowed be thy name.

James 1:5 - If any of you lack wisdom, let him ask of God, that giveth to all men liberally, and upbraideth not; and it shall be given him.

James 1:6 - But let him ask in faith, nothing wavering. For he that wavereth is like a wave of the sea driven with the wind and tossed.

Matthew 6:7 - But when ye pray, use not vain repetitions, as the heathen do: for they think that they shall be heard for their much speaking.

Luke 11:9 - And I say unto you, Ask, and it shall be given you; seek, and ye shall find; knock, and it shall be opened unto you.

Scriptures to Read and Pray When You Feel..

Ashamed	Doubtful	Lonely
● Psalm 51:1-4	● Matthew 17:14-20	● 1 Kings 19:1-18
● Psalm 119:46	● Luke 7:18-23	● Psalm 68:6
● Matthew 10:32-22	● John 20:24-29	● John 16:5-15
● Romans 1:16-17	● James 1:5-8	● Hebrews 10:25
		● Hebrews 13:5

Sick	Grief/Sorrow	Scared/Fearful
● James 5:14-16	● 2 Samuel 1:1-12	● Psalm 27:1
● 3 John 1:2	● Nehemiah 1:1-11	● Isaiah 41:13
● Isaiah 53:4-5	● Psalm 23	● 1 Corinthians 16:13
● Psalms 34:19	● Psalm 31:10, 14	● 1 John 4:18
● Matthew 10:8	● John 11:33-35	● Psalm 34:4
● Proverbs 17:22	● John 16:33	● Isaiah 41:10
● 2 Chronicles 7:14	● 1 Peter 5:7	● Proverbs 3:25-26
● 1 Peter 2:24		● 1 John 4:18

Brokenhearted/Bitter	Hurt/Rejected	Sad
● Psalm 34:18	● Isaiah 11:9	● 1 Samuel 1:15-18
● Psalm 147:3	● Luke 6:28	● Nehemiah 8:10-12
● Isaiah 61:1	● 1 Thessalonians 3:1-8	● Psalm 42:5-11
● Luke 15:11-32	● Psalm 27:9-10	● Romans 12:15
● Ephesians 4:31-32	● Psalm 77:1-12	
● Hebrews 12:14-17	● Mark 6:1-6	

Criticized	Jealous	Worried
● Proverbs 13:18	● 1 Corinthians 13:4	● Matthew 6:25-34
● Proverbs 15:31-32	● James 3:13-18	● Luke 10:38-42
● Ecclesiastes 7:5	● 1 Peter 2:1	● Philippians 4:6-9
● Titus 2:8		● 1 Peter 5:7
● James 4:11		● Psalm 46:1, 2

Promises of God

Isaiah 40:31	He gives strength to the weary.
Matthew 11:28	He will give you rest.
Isaiah 54:10	His love never fails.
Colossians 1:14	He has redeemed you.
Ephesians 1:5	He has adopted you.
Exodus 14:14	He will fight for you.
James 1:5	He gives you wisdom.
James 4:7	He protects you from evil.
1 John 1:19	Repent and He forgives
Roman 6:6	He makes you new
Luke 6:37	Forgive others and He forgives you.
Matthew 23:12	He will exalt the humble.
Deuteronomy 31:6	He will never forsake you.
John 3:16	He will set you free.
Mark 11:24	Ask in prayer and you will receive.
Philippians 4:19	He will meet all your needs.
Psalm 50:10	Call on Him and He will answer you.
Psalm 37:4	He will give what your heart desires.
Revelation 3:5	Your name will be written in the book of life, if...,
Romans 8:28	He makes all things work for your good.
Matthew 6:31	Seek the kingdom and he will provide all else.
Proverbs 3:5-6	He will make your paths straight.
Romans 8:16-17	He has prepared a place for you.
Revelation 22:12	He is coming again soon.

My Gratitude Prayer Journal

Today, I am having a great start to the day The Lord has made, in Jesus Name

Date_____

Individual I'm Praying For	Prayer Needs	Date Prayer Answered

My Gratitude List
_____
_____
_____
_____
_____
_____

Questions I Have about my studies
_____
_____
_____
_____
_____
_____
_____
_____

Today's Meditation Scripture
_____
_____
_____
_____
_____
_____
_____

Scriptures I Am Studying
_____
_____
_____
_____
_____
_____
_____
_____
_____

My Personal I Am Statement
_____
_____
_____

Vision Board Worksheet

Action Plan

As you work on your goals, create your own action items. Pay attention to how the smaller tasks align with our big goal and how each deadline builds on the last.

Sample Goal: Here, I want to launch a personal website showcasing a creative portfolio. It's currently September. I want to launch my personal creative website by mid-October.

A Goal without a plan is just a Wish

This is my goal.

- What's the goal or mission? _____

_____

- Why is it essential?_____

_____

This is my plan.

	To accomplish this goal I need to	Resources I Need	Timeline
1			
2			
3			

Push yourself across the finish line. A well-developed task list will help keep you motivated and accountable on days when you'd rather stay in bed. Be sure you set your goals to be relevant and timely.

Prayerful Coloring Pages

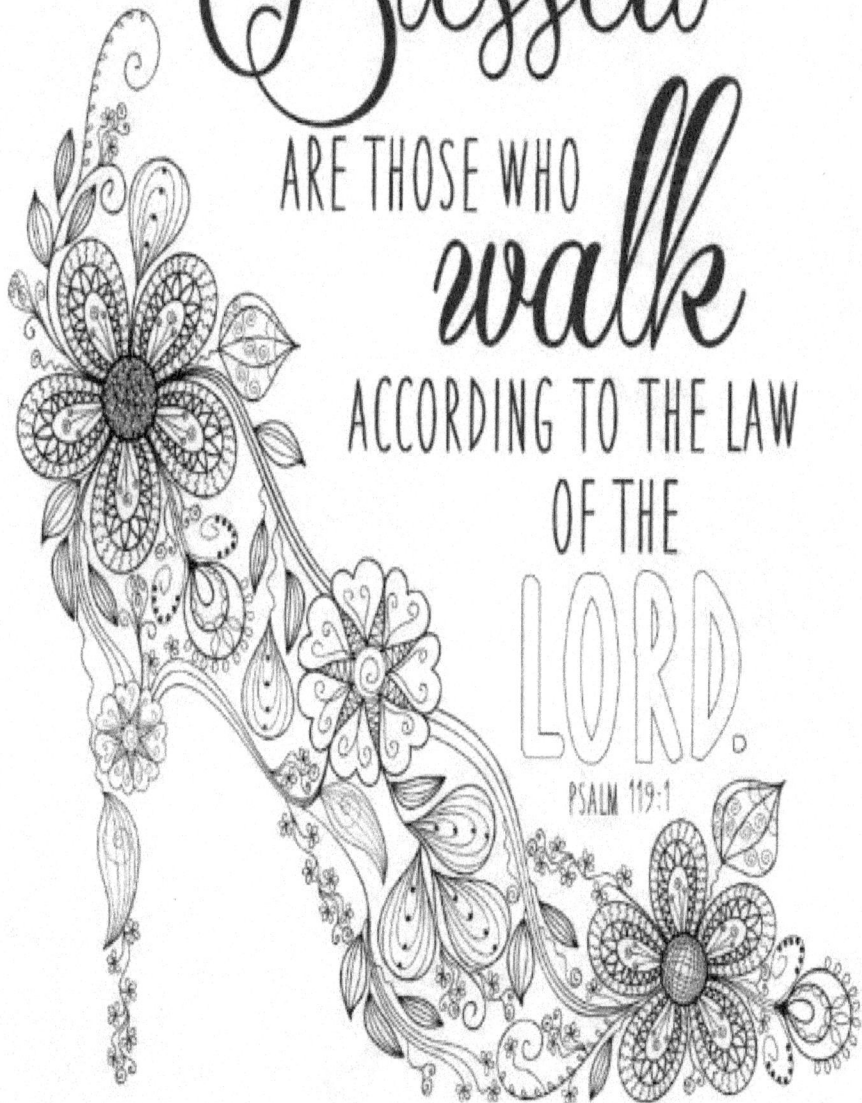

I can do all things through Christ who strengthens me. Philippians 4:13

OUR GOD is an Awesome GOD

Step Into Your Power Series

I offer a virtual or face to face workshop series based on the information in this book for women's groups. The series uses reflective thinking and writing as tools for restoration. Self-reflection is often used in education to empower people suffering from trauma and anxiety. This technique helps to begin the process of recognizing how past experiences are influencing present life. Take a break from the hustle and bustle of life to indulge in an hour of power reflection for self-care, healing, and renewal. These sessions offer a spiritual experience that combines the benefits of holistic conversation, meditation, and prayer to help participants find inner peace and balance.

Romans 12:2 "And be not conformed to this world: but be ye transformed by the renewing of your mind, that ye may prove what is that good, and acceptable, and perfect, will of God."

SELF-REFLECT, HEAL & RENEW YOUR MIND
WITH MICHELLE RHNEA

Online

ASK ABOUT THE STEP INTO YOUR POWER WORKSHOP SERIES AT MICHELLERHNEA.COM

- Session 1 Self-Reflection & Self-Care
- Session 2 Healing with Meditation on God's Word
- Session 2 Renewing and Restoring Your Mind

STEP INTO
YOUR POWER
WORKSHOP SERIES

Session 1: Self-Reflection for Self-Care

Objectives: Self-reflection is crucial because it can help you better manage your mental health. Being present with yourself and deliberately turning your attention inward to consider your thoughts, feelings, behaviors, and motivations constitute self-reflection. By actively reflecting on yourself, you can improve your grasp of who you are, your beliefs, and the reasons behind your thoughts and actions. The advantages and significance of self-reflection are discussed in this empowerment session, along with journaling exercises to help you put it into practice and apply it to your everyday life. We also discuss when self-analysis can become unhealthy and offer several coping mechanisms.

Romans 12:2 *"And be not conformed to this world: but be ye transformed by the renewing of your mind, that ye may prove what is that good, and acceptable, and perfect, will of God."*

What makes you feel calm?

How do you calm your nerves in a difficult situation?

How often do you take time alone? Is it enough? Do you need more?

How do you advocate for yourself?

How do you forgive yourself when you make a mistake?

How do you practice self-love and self-kindness?

Session 2: Healing with Meditation on The Word of God

Description

We often overestimate our own ability but underestimate The Most High's inability by doubting him and limiting his power. Yet the humble recognize that they are not God. God is all-powerful, all-knowing, and able to handle all our cares. As a humble person, you can cast all your cares on Him because you know He cares for you. To "cast" literally means to "throw." It is used to describe how the people threw their coats on the colt before Jesus rode it into Jerusalem in Luke 19:35. We should not hold onto our cares. Instead, we should throw them to our Father God who cares for us. He has big shoulders; He can handle our burdens. In this session, participants will explore ways to cast their **burdens** on God for healing.

Burden: A heavy load, a troublesome responsibility, a cause to worry.
1 Peter 5:7 - Casting all your care upon him; for he careth for you, this is the basis for this session.

Getting Started:

What does 1 Peter mean for our daily walk?

What steps can you take to improve your ability to be grateful as a common and long-term practice?

How can having an attitude of gratitude help your recharge?

What did you do that you are grateful for? What did someone else do that you are grateful for?

What did you learn you are grateful for? What did you feel that you are grateful for? Is there a difference?

Session 3: Reflection to Renew and Restore Your Mind

Inter-Personal Relationships A crucial component of self-development is self-reflection. It's a necessary skill for personal development. The practice of self-reflection involves consciously focusing inward and being present with oneself. Engaging in active self-reflection can enhance your comprehension of your identity, values, and the reasons behind your thoughts and behaviors. Self-reflection is crucial as it shapes your self-perception and promotes personal growth. Give yourself permission to free write your answers without any judgment or pressure. Learn about yourself and the way you take care of yourself. Increased sense of control: Self-reflection and being in the present moment are key components to developing health functional relationships. You may feel more rooted and in charge of your life as a result. You can strengthen your communication abilities through self-reflection, which will aid your relationships with others.

1. Are you letting matters that are out of my control stress me out?

2.How do you swap envy for joy when other people accomplish things?

3.How do you share your feelings with the people who care about you?

4.What is a good way to set limits without allowing the stress and feelings of others to lay to heavy on you? How do you put yourself first without feeling guilty?

5. How do you ask for help or support when you need it?

6. How do you make the time you spend with people more intentional?

The Battle is Not Yours

**Go to my website to sign up for
the Jeremiah 9 Woman Experience**

THE JEREMIAH 9
WOMAN
EXPERIENCE

Books in the Jeremiah 9 Woman Series

Become a Praying Woman
Step Into Your Power Study Journey
Lesson From Our Foremothers

Go to michellerhnea.com for the books in the Jeremiah 9 Woman series and more.

www.ingramcontent.com/pod-product-compliance
Lightning Source LLC
Chambersburg PA
CBHW022136080426
42734CB00006B/393